N OUR FISHING GUIDE SERIES

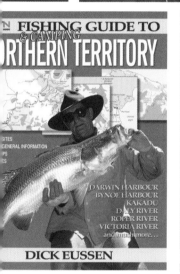

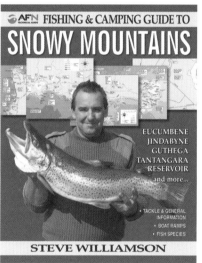

OUR FISHING & CAMPING SERIES

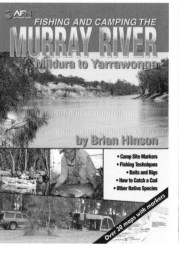

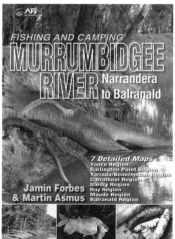

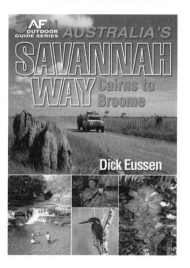

FISHING GUIDE TO
SOUTH OF SYDNEY

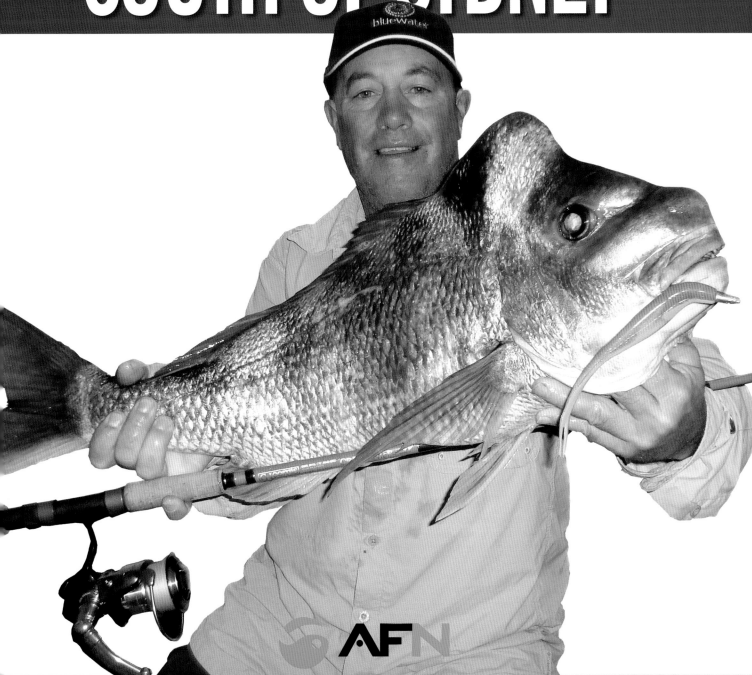

GARY BROWN

ACKNOWLEDGEMENTS

To put together an information guide of this size takes a lot of time and effort to get it all together and it is something that I have not done alone. It would be very remiss of me to not acknowledge the expertise of Alan and Vicky Perry who over the years have kept me company while fishing for tailor, Australian salmon, drummer, bream, snapper and many more fish species from the rocks and beaches of the south coast.

I would also like to thank Phil Coles and John Bell for their ongoing support, which has enabled me to bring my passion for fishing into a book of this type

Whenever I read a new book or an article the first thing I do is go through them and look at the pictures and it is these pictures that give me an insight into what the book or article is about. I have taken most of the photos in this book, but there are quite a number of them that have been supplied to me from other anglers who have spent time fishing this stretch of the NSW south coast. They are Sean from Wattos Tackle at St Marys, Scotty Lyons from Southern Sydney Fishing Tours, Andrew McGovern (Pflueger Fishing Pro) and Marc Huisken from Pure Fishing and Steve Cheng from Tropic Angler. It is with the help of their photos that I have hopefully given you an insight into what the near south coast has in store for you when you fish this area.

First published 2010

Published and distributed by
Australian Fishing Network
PO Box 544 Croydon, Victoria 3136
Telephone: (03) 9729 8788 Facsimile: (03) 9729 7833
Email: sales@afn.com.au
Website: www.afn.com.au

©Australian Fishing Network 2010

ISBN: 9781 8651 3169 6

CONTENTS

INTRODUCTION

When I was 14 years old my parents brought a block of land down at a little sea side village called Gerroa. We used to spend every weekend travelling down from Sydney to Gerroa to either go surfing or fishing while at the same time building our holiday home. It was during those early years of my life that I got the opportunity to explore the 200 kilometres of coastal shoreline, rivers, creeks, dams and land locked waterways from Wollongong to Batemans Bay.

For those of you that have never ventured to this beautiful part of the NSW coast it is something that you need to put in your bucket list of things to do. There are hundreds and hundreds of places that you can wet a line on the south coast and in this book I have put together a series of 32 maps and about 470 fishing spots to help you to explore the near south coast of NSW.

Places like Bass Point, just south of Shellharbour. This rock finger of land that juts out into the passing currents, is a natural gathering ground for many different species. Some of which are, snapper, bream, drummer, tailor, Australian salmon, pike, silver trevally, kingfish, bonito and groper, just to name a few.

If rock fishing is not to your liking you may like to explore the Shoalhaven River from either the shore or out of a boat. This is southern NSW's largest and most significant river that rises between Braidwood and Araluen, flowing north and then east for over 400 kilometres, entering the sea near Greenwell Point.

Now when it comes to lakes, you may like to visit the little township of Lake Conjola that is situated just north of Ulladulla right on the coast. The lake empties into the Tasman Sea and most of the time is crystal clear. The lower section of the lake has extensive sand flats which are great for large dusky flathead, whiting and bream and is the largest lake in the area almost permanently open to the sea. However, the sea entrance in dangerous and not navigable. There are 3 boat ramps around the lake for access for small and large boats.

There is nothing like the feeling you get when standing on a beach as the sun rises over the horizon, while the waves of the surf lap at your feet. One of my favourite places to do this is at Racecourse Beach at Bawley. There is plenty on offer here for the beach and rock angler. It is a place where you could base yourself and explore both to the north and south.

It has taken me a few years and plenty of blood, sweat and tears to put this fishing guide together. With its 32 maps and over 470 fishing spots I hope that this information will also help you to expand your fishing horizons to those areas that I have fished since I was 14, and am still fishing with my many fishing friends to this day.

Fishing Guide to South of Sydney
Key for map positioning

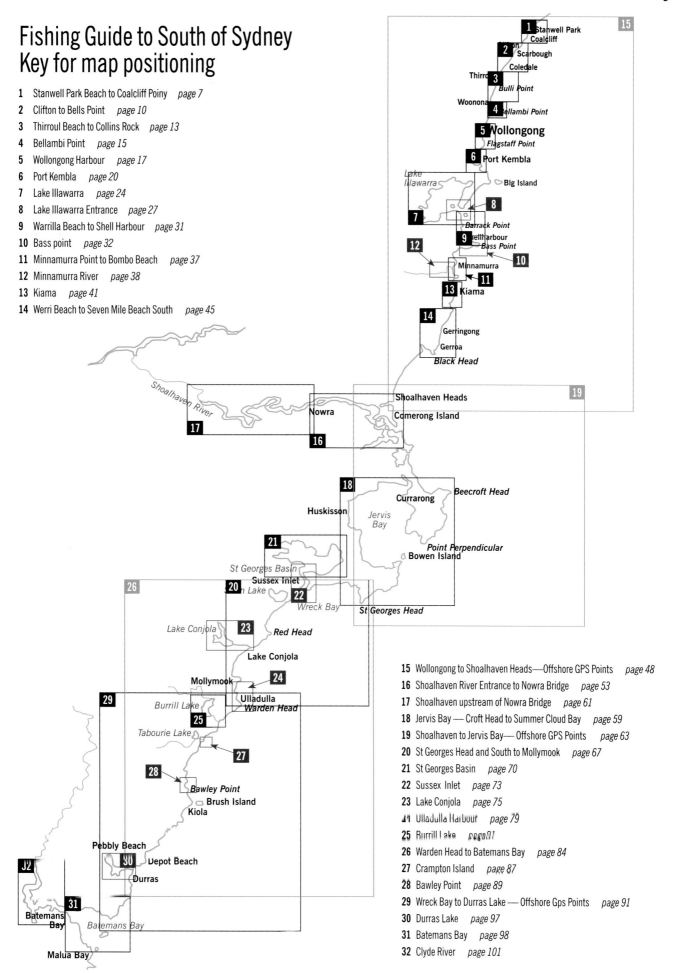

CHAPTER 1
WOLLONGONG
Stanwell Park Beach to Bass Point

Starting from the south and travelling north you have Port Kembla, Bellambi Point, Woonona Beach, Bulli Beach, Sandon Point and then Bulli Point.

With a culturally-diverse population of around 200,000 people, Wollongong is ranked as Australia's 10th largest city, and is located just 80 km south of the centre of Sydney, our largest city. Yet, despite this proximity to these major urban concentrations, and the presence of more than five million people living within a few hours drive, this region of NSW still has much to offer the local and visiting angler alike.

Wollongong is set on a narrow strip of coastal plain bounded by the very steep Illawarra escarpment to the west and the blue Pacific Ocean or Tasman Sea to the east. Because of these physical limitations, "The 'Gong", as it's popularly known, is very much a linear city, stretching in a thin, virtually unbroken urban line from Helensburgh in the north to the shores of Lake Illawarra and Windang to the south, where it effectively links up with the northern side of the fast-growing Shellharbour metropolitan region.

Despite its relatively large and densely-packed population, Wollongong's natural environment remains one of its greatest assets. The escarpment dominates the landscape of the area, rising abruptly from the sea to altitudes of over 300 metres in places. Its heavily forested slopes provide a spectacular backdrop for Wollongong's suburbs and a valuable corridor for native flora and fauna. National Parks, State Recreation Areas, pockets of sub-tropical rainforest, 17 patrolled beaches and Lake Illawarra all add to the appeal of Wollongong's landscape and offer its inhabitants the opportunity to pursue a diverse range of outdoor recreational activities, including, of course, fishing!

Another of the area's most valuable natural assets is busy Port Kembla Harbour. This is the deepest port on the eastern seaboard, providing local and regional industry with excellent export links to the rest of the world, and servicing the busy steel mills that this part of Wollongong is most famous for. However, be aware that, because of its commercial and strategic importance, large portions of this working harbour are strictly off-limits to recreational users, including anglers. Luckily, there are lots of alternative fishing venues to choose from.

Just to the north of Wollongong you will come across a small, but very productive beach at Stanwell Park. There is plenty of parking and it is only a short five minute walk to the beach where you can target tailor, Australian salmon, yellowfin bream and whiting. Travelling south to Bass Point you will come across around 28 beaches, which I have listed in this chapter and as you read on you will find that some of these beaches produce tailor and Australian salmon, some are better to target jewfish and sharks, whilst at others you can chase yellowfin bream and whiting.

If beach fishing is not your scene and you prefer the excitement of fishing off the rocks you can target all of the above fish species, plus bonito, tuna, kingfish, drummer, groper and luderick. There is some great high speed spinning to be had off the rocks and breakwalls in this stretch of the coast

For those anglers who prefer to just fish from the shore or out of a boat you could always try drifting for dusky flathead in Lake Illawarra, chase squid and mullet off the breakwalls at Port Kembla and Wollongong Harbour or just while away the time watching the float when targeting luderick.

Now if you decide to spend a while on this stretch of the south coast you could always visit the local tourist information centre and check out what is going on. There are plenty of places to go bush walking, bike riding, dining out or just relaxing while having a barbeque or picnic.

MAP 1   STANWELL PARK BEACH TO COALCLIFF POINT

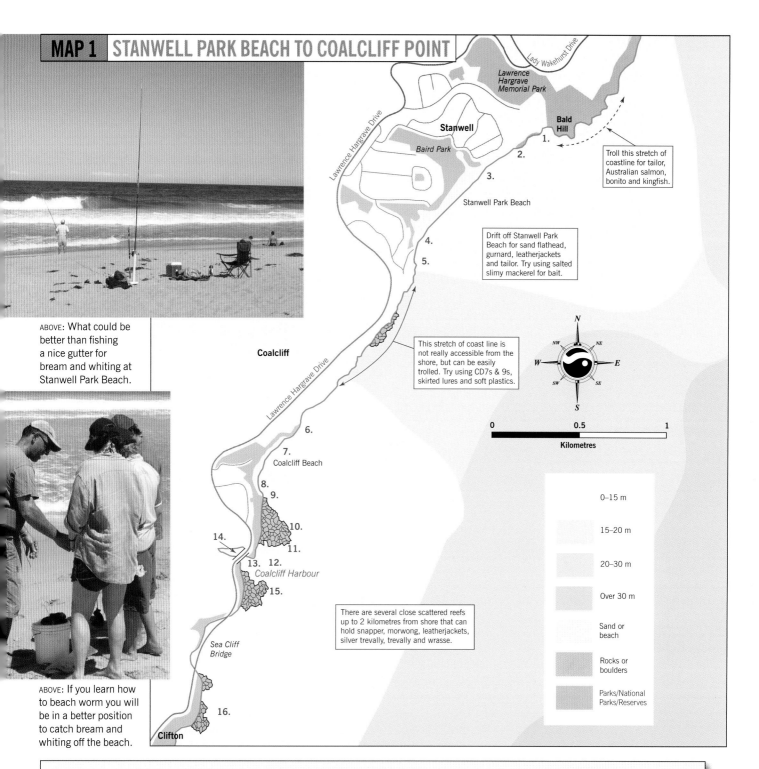

ABOVE: What could be better than fishing a nice gutter for bream and whiting at Stanwell Park Beach.

ABOVE: If you learn how to beach worm you will be in a better position to catch bream and whiting off the beach.

Lawrence Hargrave Memorial Park

Stanwell

Baird Park

Bald Hill

1.

2.

3.

Stanwell Park Beach

4.

5.

Troll this stretch of coastline for tailor, Australian salmon, bonito and kingfish.

Drift off Stanwell Park Beach for sand flathead, gurnard, leatherjackets and tailor. Try using salted slimy mackerel for bait.

Coalcliff

Lawrence Hargrave Drive

This stretch of coast line is not really accessible from the shore, but can be easily trolled. Try using CD7s & 9s, skirted lures and soft plastics.

6.

7.

Coalcliff Beach

8.

9.

10.

14.

11.

13. 12.

Coalcliff Harbour

15.

There are several close scattered reefs up to 2 kilometres from shore that can hold snapper, morwong, leatherjackets, silver trevally, trevally and wrasse.

Sea Cliff Bridge

16.

Clifton

	0–15 m
	15–20 m
	20–30 m
	Over 30 m
	Sand or beach
	Rocks or boulders
	Parks/National Parks/Reserves

0   0.5   1
Kilometres

MAP 1 STANWELL PARK BEACH TO COALCLIFF POINT

Stanwell Park is situated just south of the boundaries of the Royal National Park. The rock and beach fishing spots you can access from here and down to Coalcliff Point are renowned for great fishing. Most of the fishing spots I have listed are easily accessed by car and then by foot. Due to the type of rock terrain you will be fishing from I would suggest that you wear a pair of rubber sole joggers or a pair of shoes that have cleats on them. A backpack is also an essential piece of equipment, as it will give you the freedom to move from spot to spot.

Even though many of the spots will have bait there that you can use, it would be advisable to take prawns, nippers, fillets of fish, pilchards and garfish. Live bait can be caught at most of the spots, and the beaches are always worth a try for beach worms on a falling tide.

1.1   THE PLAQUE

This area will need to be fished in small to moderate seas and care will need to be taken at all times. It is a place that sometimes cannot be reached on those high, high tides and a sea with any groundswell at all. You can target bream, drummer, silver trevally, snapper, and Australian salmon and tailor here. The fish will be either in close under the white wash or further out on the sandy pockets that are in between the boulders.

There is also a small beach at this location that can be fished for bream, sand whiting, tailor and Australian salmon. Try using whole pilchards for the tailor and Australian salmon and either half pilchards, cunje, peeled prawns, pink nippers, mullet or tuna fillets for most of the other fish species found there. I have also caught a couple of small groper and snapper here amongst the rocks.

1.2   THE BOULDERS

Where the sand meets the rocks at the northern end of Stanwell Park beach you will find that there are also a few big boulders that are out in the surf area. It is here that you will need to target the bream silver trevally, dart and small drummer. Normally I would fish with a long leader, but due to the fact that there are a number of boulders here you will need to shorten your leader to about 50cm or have the ball sinker right down on the bait. You could also try using the paternoster rig with a couple of hooks. You can also catch salmon and tailor here as well.

Best baits are half pilchards, cunje, peeled prawns, pink nippers, mullet and tuna fillets for bream, silver trevally, dart and small drummer. Use either whole pilchards or garfish for the tailor and salmon.

1.3   NORTH STANWELL PARK BEACH

Due to the fact that this beach is fully exposed to a southerly swell and wind it can change its formations in a blink of an eye. This should not discourage you from going down there to throw a line for mulloway and whiting from November through to the end of April. Salmon, tailor, bream and the odd dart can be caught here from May through to the beginning of spring. It is best fished around dawn and dusk, but can produce some great results after there has been a bit of a sea.

Try whole pilchards and garfish for the tailor and salmon, fillets of mullet and whole squid for the mulloway. Pink nippers, beach and blood worms, pilly tails and pieces of mullet and tuna are good baits for bream, whiting and dart. It is a beach that will fire on one day and then be dead the next. So patience is a virtue.

1.4   THE PARKING LOT

The area where you will need to stand is only a short walk from the southern car park. It is where the sand meets the rocks and the rig I prefer to use has the ball sinker directly on top of the bait you are using. Bream, tailor, salmon and the odd drummer will frequent this area on a rising tide. The first hour of the falling tide is also a good time to fish here. Best times seems to be dawn and dusk.

1.5   SOUTHERN CLIFFS

This area is not fishable in any heavy seas, but is best fished after there has been a bit of a sea running. You will need to cast out wide of the rock and boulders for tailor, salmon, bream and mulloway. Once you get there you will find a few areas that have been carved out of the rocks for you to stand on. You could also try fishing with the ball sinker directly down onto the bait for bream in and around the boulders.

What a fantastic sunrise on a south coast beach.

Looking north from Coalcliff to Stanwell Park you will notice a small reef break. This reef is directly out from the surf club at Coalcliff. Here you can target bream, silver trevally and snapper from the beach.

1.6   NORTH COALCLIFF

This is not an area that is fished a lot, but it is a place that can produce some great catches. You will need to walk around the rocks to the first prominent rocky finger that comes into view. It is here that you can fish for tailor, salmon, snapper and mulloway during the early parts of the day and well into the night.

Bream and silver trevally can be berleyed up here during the winter months. You will need to cast out onto the gravel and sandy bottom for the best results. Try using one rod with a paternoster rig and another one with a running ball sinker and a leader of about a metre in length.

1.7   SURF CLUB

Directly out in front of the Coalcliff Surf Life Saving Club there is a small, but very productive reef. There will usually be a deeper channel on either side of the reef and this is where you will need to direct your long cast. I have fished here during the winter months for snapper and bream on a falling tide. To help me get out to these areas I have tied a small party balloon to the line and have let the offshore wind take the bait out the required distance.

During the summer months you will need to target, bream, whiting, dart, flathead and the odd silver trevally here. Best baits have been beach and blood worms, pink nippers, peeled prawns and pilly tails.

1.8   COALCLIFF BEACH

The southern end of the beach is a great place to fish after there has been a bit of a southerly swell and there is plenty of white water foaming up in the corner. Bream, salmon, tailor and drummer will school up under the suds. Try using a paternoster rig and either pink nippers, peeled prawns, cunje, abalone and chicken gut on a rising and falling tide. If you are prepared to put in the time and effort you can even get a mulloway or two here during the summer months.

During the winter months you will need to beef up you gear as there are plenty of drummer that feed in the area. Abalone gut, cunje and peeled prawns are the gun baits for here.

1.9   SWIMMING POOL

If you are after a few bream and luderick you can try fishing off the back of the rock pool at the southern end of the beach. It is not a place to be when there is a big sea running. Make sure that you berley with bread and fish with either a bobby cork or a stem float. This will usually keep your bait away from the snags that are found here.

1.10   SHALLOW GUTTER

As you are walking out onto Coalcliff Point you will notice that there is a gutter on the northern side. During the lower parts of the tide there is not much water in here and is best fished a couple of hours before the top of the tide and for about an hour as the tide falls. Bream, drummer, luderick and silver trevally will frequent this gutter. Care will need to be taken here as the waves can and will break over the front of the rocks. Try directing your baits to land near the boulders, as this is where the drummer and bream will seek out their next meal.

1.11   THE LEDGE

I have caught blue morwong, snapper, kingfish, leatherjackets, bream, salmon, tailor, drummer and even striped tuna off this part of the Coalcliff Point. But, one thing that you will need to do at all times is keep an eye on the seas. I have seen and heard of a number of anglers that have been washed in here. I have also been there when a couple of anglers were not washed in, but were dragged back across the rocks. They were lucky, but they did loose most of their gear and bait. It is also a great place to get your live bait, luderick and drummer.

1.12   SOUHERN LEDGE

The southern tip of this very flat platform can be very dangerous to fish in heavy seas. So you will need to assess the conditions that are running at the time. A long cast will get you onto a bottom that has a mixture of shale, broken reef and sand. Here you can get bream, snapper, morwong, kingfish and the odd silver trevally. The best rig to use here is a paternoster with either strips of tuna, mullet or mackerel for bait. You could also try using squid whole or in strips.

In close to the ledge you will be able to berley up garfish, yellowtail, sweep, leatherjackets and luderick. After you have cast the rig out wide, I would suggest that you fish as light as the conditions will allow for trevally and bream. You could also try casting out metal lures for Australian salmon, tailor and bonito.

For those of you using live bait you need to suspend it under a bobby cork or a balloon. If not you could always put one on a paternoster rig and cast it out wide.

The southern end of Coalcliff rock platform.

Dart are common fish species that are caught off Stanwell Park Beach.

1.13   KELPY BAY

When the front of the platform gets very crowded this is a place to come and fish for drummer, luderick, bream and silver trevally. I will put my berley into an onion bag and suspend it just in the water. In that way the berley will not disperse all over the place, and will keep the fish at my feet.

1.14   PROTECTION CORNER

When the seas are big and it is too dangerous to fish out the front you can get yourself up high and fish for tailor, salmon and bream on the rising tide, but you will still need to take care when fishing here. Try fishing with whole pilchards or garfish suspended under a bobby cork. If not you could always cast out a whole pilchard or garfish on a set of 5/0 ganged hooks and slowly retrieve it back towards the shore.

1.15   BREAM ALLEY

This small but very productive corner is a great place to fish for bream when there is a westerly wind blowing. The water will become very clear, but if you have a steady stream of berley you will get the bream on the bite. Best baits have been bread, pink nippers, peeled prawns and strips of mullet. This is also a reliable ground to get live baits like yellowtail, mullet and garfish.

1.16   THE WASHES

Access by foot is extremely difficult, so this spot is best fished from a boat when the seas are flat. I prefer to fish with my 3.6 metre Mag Bream rod and Alvey reel. The reel is loaded up with 6 kilo line and I use royal red prawns, abalone gut, pink nippers and cunje for bait. It is not uncommon to catch bream, silver trevally, drummer, luderick, tailor and snapper here during the winter months.

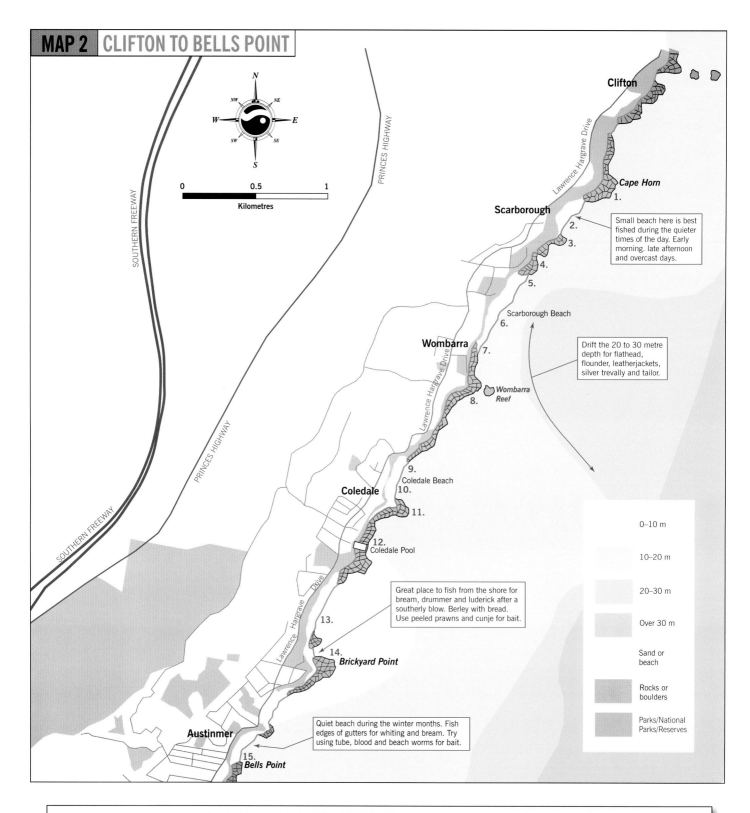

MAP 2 CLIFTON TO BELLS POINT

Clifton

Cape Horn

Scarborough

1.

2.

Small beach here is best fished during the quieter times of the day. Early morning. late afternoon and overcast days.

3.

4.

5.

Scarborough Beach

6.

Wombarra 7.

Drift the 20 to 30 metre depth for flathead, flounder, leatherjackets, silver trevally and tailor.

Wombarra Reef

8.

9.

Coledale Beach

10.

Coledale

11.

12.

Coledale Pool

Great place to fish from the shore for bream, drummer and luderick after a southerly blow. Berley with bread. Use peeled prawns and cunje for bait.

13.

14.

Brickyard Point

Quiet beach during the winter months. Fish edges of gutters for whiting and bream. Try using tube, blood and beach worms for bait.

Austinmer

15.

Bells Point

PRINCES HIGHWAY

SOUTHERN FREEWAY

Lawrence Hargrave Drive

0   0.5   1

Kilometres

0–10 m

10–20 m

20–30 m

Over 30 m

Sand or beach

Rocks or boulders

Parks/National Parks/Reserves

MAP 2 CLIFTON TO BELLS POINT

Situated in the small northern coast town of Scarborough, this small beach offers fantastic views of the coastline and the cliffs that lie above. There are parklands close by for families to use for picnicking. Scarborough is located 21km North of Wollongong CBD.

The surf club operates a small and unique grassy campsite that borders right onto the golden sand. Coledale Beach is beautifully sandwiched between the rolling blue surf of the Pacific and the green tree canopy of the Illawarra escarpment.

Just one hour south of Sydney CBD, the small beachside village of Coledale is accessed by the spectacular Grand Pacific Drive via the stunning Sea Cliff Bridge. Well serviced from Sydney and the south coast by city rail trains and with regular local bus services. The stunning beach is bordered north and south by rocky outcrops that protect the beach from the worst of the weather, as well as offering excellent fishing spots. The beach is a great surfing spot, with the right conditions offering nice right and left hand breaks. Never as crowded as other comparable surf spots, Coledale Beach is a great location to enjoy the beach, swim, surf, fish, dive or just sit back, enjoy the views and sound of the surf at your doorstep. Regular visits by dolphins playing just off the beach and close views of migrating humpback and southern right whales just add to the experience.

2.1 CAPE HORN POINT

This is a great place to chase bream, trevally, drummer and tailor on a falling tide. It can be very snaggy at this spot so you will need to fish as light as possible. Whole or half pilchards and garfish are the go. You can get a number of squid here at times, so don't forget to take that squid jig.

2.2 BEACH

If you are looking to take the family out for a beach fish for bream and whiting this is the place to go, but you will need to use a paternoster rig and don't forget to take the pink nipper, beach and blood worms. They will get you the best results

2.3 RECREATION RESERVE

This small, but sometimes productive point is worth a shot for bream on a rising tide. You will need to cast out a fair way to get onto the sandy area. The occasional big silver trevally is caught here as well.

2.4 NOBBIES

Great place to target bream, silver trevally and drummer on a rising tide. Leatherjackets and squid are also caught here, but you will need to fish as light as the conditions will allow you to.

2.5 ILLAWARRA PARK

To gain access to this spot you will need to drive along Hargrave Drive until you get to Cliff Road. Here you can fish for bream and whiting at the top of the tide. Beach and blood worms seem to work the best, but you could also try using strips of mullet and tuna for the bream. The odd sand flathead is caught here as well.

2.6 SCARBOROUGH BEACH

This is a fairly large beach that attracts bream, whiting, silver trevally, tailor, Australian salmon and jewfish on a rising tide. Best fished either just as the sun is coming up, late in the afternoon when the shadows have started to form on the water, or on an overcast day.

2.7 MARTIN DUNSTER PARK

Best fished after there has been a big sea running and it has just started to quieten down a bit. Try using a paternoster rig or a leader of about half a metre in length. Strips of mullet and tuna are worth a shot from here for bream, drummer and silver trevally.

Where does one start? There are so many great places to fish on this stretch of coastline north of Wollongong.

2.8   WOMBARRA REEF

This small rock platform can be easily accessed by following the coast road and turning off into the ocean pool road. You can cast off the end of the pool at high tide for bream on either beach or blood worms. Try fishing the northern side of the island on a rising tide for drummer and bream. Best fished in the late afternoon. The right hand side of the point fishes well for leatherjackets, silver trevally, bream, drummer and luderick. A long cast from here will usually get you amongst the tailor, Australian salmon and the odd jewfish.

2.9   NORTH COLEDALE CORNER

The set of rocks at this end of Coledale is fairly heavily fished, due to the fact that there is easy access from the cark park. Don't let this deter you from fishing here for bream, silver trevally, tailor Australian salmon, luderick and drummer on a rising tide. Fish off the high rocks on the right hand side for luderick, bream and drummer. Cast over the old storm water drain that used to empty out for bream, groper and leatherjackets. On the north end of this rock platform there is a large hole in the middle of the platform. This is best fished in rough seas and when the tide is at its highest.

2.10   COLEDALE BEACH

This is a nice little beach that is best fished on a rising tide a couple of hours before the sun sets. Bream, whiting and tailor can be caught here. Try using pink nippers, beach and blood worms, half pillies and strips of mullet. I have found that the winter months produce the best results

2.11   SOUTH COLEDALE POINT

Fish off this point on a rising tide for bream, jewfish and whiting. You will need to get a fairly long cast in so that you set the baits on the sandy area. In close to the shore there are a number of snags so you will need to fish a light as possible of suspend your baits under a bobby cork.

2.12   COLEDALE POOL

Fish along this ledge towards the beach on a rising tide at night for bream, silver trevally and whiting. The wash running off the shallow reef at the point forms a great place to cast lightly weighted bait. There is also a small patch of boulders that are worth a shot for drummer and luderick on a falling tide. Where the cunje beds starts is a good place to chase drummer and bream with pink nippers, peeled prawns or cunje.

2.13   FREW MEMORIAL PARK

The corner of the beach here is worth a shot for bream, whiting and silver trevally on a rising tide. If you try fishing this same spot just after there has been a bit of a sea with whole pilchards and garfish you are in with a chance for tailor and Australian salmon.

2.14   BRICKYARD POINT

Reached by an easy walk from the car park on both sides of the headland, this point offers anglers most varieties of rock fishing. Try fishing the higher rocks into the small gutters for bream, silver trevally, luderick and the odd drummer.

The left hand side of the area is usually good for luderick.

For those of you who like to chase groper, large drummer and leatherjackets you can cast towards the reef just out in front with crabs, cunje and peeled prawns. Just to the left of this spot you can fish a small and shallow gutter at high tide for bream, silver trevally and drummer. Just north of this area there is a set of higher rocks that can be fished quite easily on a rising tide in the late afternoon when the shadows start to appear on the water.

2.15   AUSTINMER BOAT HARBOUR

Although access to this point can become difficult from the north side in big seas, it still offers anglers good fishing and it is in easy walking distance from the car park. There are a number of large gutters where you can fish for luderick, bream and drummer with cunje, green weed, cabbage and peeled blue tailed prawns. You can also cast from the low rocks out the front for Australian salmon, snapper and tailor. The northern side of the point fishes well for bream on a rising and falling tide. Try using peeled prawns and pink nippers for bait.

BELOW: Brickyard Point at Austinmer can produce drummer like this one if you fish light and use berley.

MAP 3 THIRROUL BEACH TO COLLINS ROCK

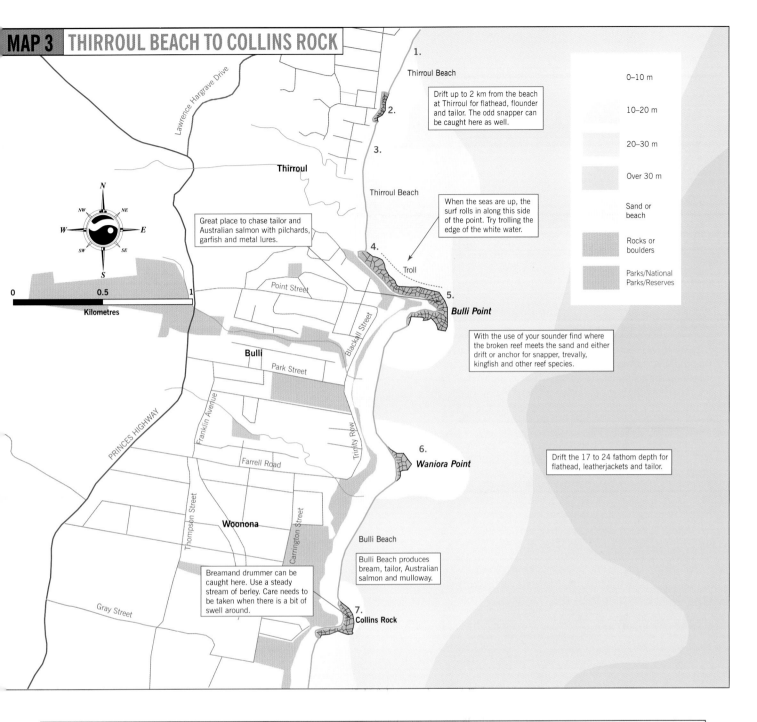

0–10 m

10–20 m

20–30 m

Over 30 m

Sand or beach

Rocks or boulders

Parks/National Parks/Reserves

1. Thirroul Beach

Drift up to 2 km from the beach at Thirroul for flathead, flounder and tailor. The odd snapper can be caught here as well.

2.

3.

Thirroul Beach

When the seas are up, the surf rolls in along this side of the point. Try trolling the edge of the white water.

4.

Troll

5.

Bulli Point

With the use of your sounder find where the broken reef meets the sand and either drift or anchor for snapper, trevally, kingfish and other reef species.

6. **Waniora Point**

Drift the 17 to 24 fathom depth for flathead, leatherjackets and tailor.

Bulli Beach

Bulli Beach produces bream, tailor, Australian salmon and mulloway.

Breamand drummer can be caught here. Use a steady stream of berley. Care needs to be taken when there is a bit of swell around.

7. **Collins Rock**

Great place to chase tailor and Australian salmon with pilchards, garfish and metal lures.

Thirroul

Point Street

Bulli

Park Street

Farrell Road

Woonona

Gray Street

Lawrence Hargrave Drive

PRINCES HIGHWAY

Franklin Avenue

Thompson Street

Carrington Street

Blackall Street

Trinity Row

N
NW NE
W E
SW SE
S

0   0.5   1
Kilometres

MAP 3 THIRROUL BEACH TO COLLINS ROCK

The town of Thirroul, once a coal mining settlement, has a village-like aspect to it and is situated in between Woonona and Austinmer, around an hour and a half from Sydney. It has become a desirable and popular commuter region for Sydneysiders and makes for a quiet beachside retreat.

Thirroul boasts a great surfing beach, which in summer is popular with locals and Sydneysiders alike. Opposite the promenade and parkland is Thirroul Pool. The town is also the home of Iron Men, Darren and Dean Mercer. Thirroul Beach is the resting place of the famous shipwreck "Amy", which was wrecked off this coast in 1898. For a perfect picnic day out, head to Thirroul Beach Reserve and the neighbouring Tingara Park which provide quiet shady picnic grounds.

3.1   THIRROUL BEACH – NORTH

I have found that the northern end of Thirroul beach has fished the best for me on a rising tide and the first two hours of the falling tide. Australian salmon, tailor, bream and sand whiting frequent this beach. You will need to locate the deeper gutters and direct your cast towards the edges of the white water for the best results. If you like chasing jewfish off the beach I would suggest that you pick a high tide that coincides with either the early morning period or just before the sun sets. Try using half or whole slabs of mullet, slimy mackerel or salmon for bait.

3.2   MIDDLE ROCKS

This is mainly a high tide spot for chasing bream and the odd whiting on a falling tide. The first two hours seem to produce the better results. Beach and blood worms are the go. At this small set of rocks it is always worth chucking out a few metal lures for Australian salmon and tailor during those low light periods.

3.3   THIRROUL BEACH – SOUTH

This section of Thirroul beach is worth a shot for bream and whiting during the summer months, while during the autumn to winter months I would target Australian salmon and tailor with whole pilchards on a set of ganged hooks. Try berleying the beach at the same time you are fishing as this will increase your chances of getting amongst a few fish.

3.4   THE EDGE

The depth of the water here will vary a lot and this is due to the rocks being exposed to the elements. I have found it best to fish here when there is a bit more in the depth of the water and when there is a bit more white water about.

3.5   BULLI POINT

There are only a couple of hundred metres to walk from the car park at the surf club to the rocks where bream, silver trevally, drummer, groper, Australian salmon, tailor and leatherjacket can be caught. Fish off the high rocks and into one of the many washes that are found there. You can also cast a line from the left hand corner of the pool for a number of different species, especially bream and small drummer.

3.6   WANIORA POINT

The swell will wrap around this point when the seas are up so care will need to be taken when fishing this point. Fish as light as the conditions will allow for bream, silver trevally, drummer and luderick. Australian salmon, tailor and bonito will frequent this point when there is a medium swell running. Try using peeled blue tailed prawns and pilly tails for the bream and trevally and whole pilchards and garfish for the pelagics.

3.7   COLLINS ROCK

Not a big rock platform, but can at times still produce good bags of bream and drummer on a rising tide. Make sure that you do have a steady stream of berley in the water.

BELOW: Bellambi, Woonona, Bulli and Sandon Point Beaches.

MAP 4 BELLAMBI POINT

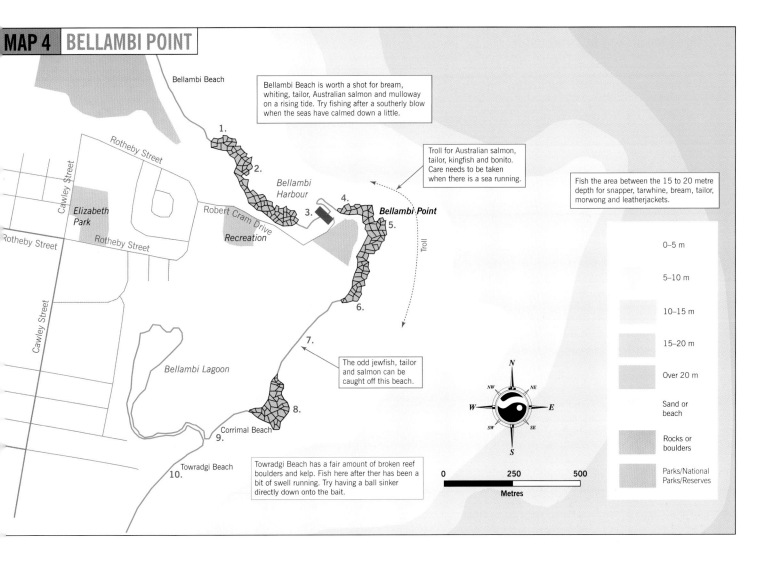

Bellambi Beach

Bellambi Beach is worth a shot for bream, whiting, tailor, Australian salmon and mulloway on a rising tide. Try fishing after a southerly blow when the seas have calmed down a little.

Troll for Australian salmon, tailor, kingfish and bonito. Care needs to be taken when there is a sea running.

Fish the area between the 15 to 20 metre depth for snapper, tarwhine, bream, tailor, morwong and leatherjackets.

Rotheby Street

Cawley Street

Elizabeth Park

Bellambi Harbour

Robert Cram Drive

Recreation

Rotheby Street

Rotheby Street

Cawley Street

Bellambi Point

Troll

Bellambi Lagoon

The odd jewfish, tailor and salmon can be caught off this beach.

Corrimal Beach

Towradgi Beach

Towradgi Beach has a fair amount of broken reef boulders and kelp. Fish here after ther has been a bit of swell running. Try having a ball sinker directly down onto the bait.

0–5 m
5–10 m
10–15 m
15–20 m
Over 20 m
Sand or beach
Rocks or boulders
Parks/National Parks/Reserves

N NW NE W E SW SE S

0 250 500
Metres

MAP 4 BELLAMBI POINT

Bellambi Creek and a low fore dune occupy much of the southern back beach, with Bellambi Surf Club lying behind the creek, and linked to the beach by a walkway. The creek runs behind the beach down to the southern rocks where swimming and kiddies' pools are located. A bike path links the two Surf Clubs. The protection from east and south east swell afforded by Bellambi Point reduces wave height down the southern half of the beach, averaging from 1 to 0.5 m. However it does receive the summer north east waves and winds which average between 1 and 1.5 m. The beach usually has an attached bar with rip frequency and intensity decreasing to the south, except during north east conditions, which will generate strong rips all the way down the beach.

4.1   BELLAMBI BEACH

This is a great little beach to fish just after there has been a bit of a blow from the south for tailor, Australian salmon and yellowfin bream. During the warmer months of the year you can target whiting and the odd sand flathead here with whitebait and half pilchards. You could also try using pink nippers, beach and blood worms.

4.2   BREAM ROCKS

Now, as the name suggests this is a very good spot to chase bream about two hours either side of the top of the tide. I have got my best results here while fishing only with a double 0 ball sinker that is directly down onto the hook. Not a good spot to fish if the seas are running. Try earlier morning or later in the afternoon.

4.3   SQUID BAY

Not only can you target squid in this bay, you can also chase bream, luderick and tailor. Especially if the prevailing conditions are from the south. There is a three-laned boat ramp nestled in the corner which gives you access to the open seas, but you will need to be careful when launching your boat here as there can be a big tidal surge when the seas are running. If you are going to launch from this boat ramp you will need to check out the Admiralty charts for the varying depths, bomboras and shallow reefs. There is a small break wall that is adjacent to the boat ramp car park and it is off this small break wall you could teach the youngsters to fish.

4.4   BELLAMBI BREAKWALL

Care needs to be taken when fishing off the break wall on the northern side of the ramp when the seas are up, but you can target Australian salmon, tailor, bream, drummer, luderick and silver trevally from the wall. Fish the wash where the wall meets the main rock shelf for bream and drummer. You will need to have a steady stream of berley running to keep the fish in the area. Try fishing the washes at the end of the wall for bream, drummer and groper. Tailor, Australian salmon, kingfish and snapper will usually respond well to bait suspended under a bobby cork.

This boat ramp offers a four laned ramp with excellent amenities, including parking for about eighty cars and trailer, fish cleaning tables, boat washing area and a holding jetty.

4.5 BELLAMBI POINT

This point has a water depth that ranges from two to five meters and is quite sheltered due to the fact that there is a small reef complex that runs out to sea for about two kilometres. There is a maze of cunje covered outcrops and breaking reefs that are separated by gutters, sand and gravel patches. Bream, silver trevally, snapper, drummer, silver trevally and even kingfish can be caught from here when the conditions are right.

4.6 THE PIPE

The pipe protrudes out to sea about 90 to 100 metres and used to be the local effluent outfall and can be a bit smelly at times. The pipe itself is quite slippery and care needs to be taken when fishing here. Bream, silver trevally, groper, tailor and Australian salmon are worth chasing here. Whole or half pilchards and garfish are worth a try as bait. You could also try using beach and blood worms, nippers and strips of mullet or tuna for bait.

This spot is one of the places that I will always wear some kind of waterproof covering as the waves can splash you a fair bit when fishing here. Directly out in front of the pipes is worth a cast for very large drummer, groper and snapper. Large trevally and jewfish can also be caught here as well.

4.7 RECREATION AREA

Jewfish, stingrays and sharks can be caught here during the night. During the day I have caught mainly yellowfin bream, whiting and tailor off the beach.

ABOVE: Alvey reels, hungry bags, bream and drummer go hand in hand when fishing off the rocks.

4.8 LUDERICK ALLEY

As the name suggests I have found this spot to be a great producer of luderick. Try fishing a couple of hours either side of the top of the tide with green weed, cabbage, peeled prawns, pink nippers and even give cunje a go.

4.9 CORMINAL BEACH

If you like chasing jewfish, sharks and rays you could try targeting them after dark off this beach. There are usually a number of deep holes and gutters found on this beach. During the day you could target bream and whiting, and in the morning and late afternoons you could cast out a whole pilchard or garfish on a set of ganged hooks for tailor and Australian salmon.

4.10 TOWRADGI BEACH

This is a very popular surf beach, but don't let this deter you from having a throw for tailor, Australian salmon, yellowfin bream and the odd whiting or two. There are a number of small reefy outcrops off the beach, so you will need to use as light a sinker as the fishing conditions will allow. You could also try using a paternoster rig. The rocks at the northern end of the beach are worth a shot for drummer during the winter months and you could try for luderick on the southern end. Best baits would be whole peeled blue tailed prawns, half and whole pilchards, cunje and strips of tuna or mackerel.

Octopus make great bait for kingfish, snapper and mulloway when fishing off the rocks.

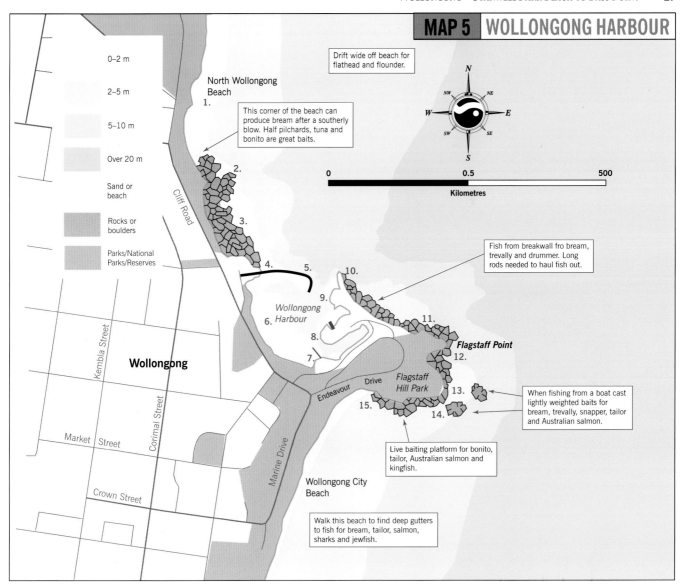

MAP 5 WOLLONGONG HARBOUR

Wollongong Harbour is situated 80km south of Sydney on the Australian east coast. It is the only point on the east coast to have two lighthouses.

With the expansion out of Sydney in the early 1800s, Wollongong Harbour was developed to serve the new township of Wollongong and the Illawarra region. In the 1860s work on the harbour included the construction of a basin and breakwater. At this time "... at the end of the pier a red light was fixed to guide boats into the harbour."

In 1869 tenders were invited for the construction of lighthouses at Wollongong and Ulladulla. Manufactured in England, shipped to Australia and assembled, construction of the Wollongong light began in November 1870 and although completed in March 1871, it stood unfinished until the lantern arrived from England in June 1871. More delays occurred until finally it was brought into permanent use on 1st March 1872. The lantern was manufactured by Chance & Co Birmingham England and was described in 1873 as being "... a fixed Dioptric system of the 4th Order with a fixed red light." The original apparatus was dismantled around 1970, as it was proposed to use this at Eden. The light was permanently extinguished in 1974.

5.1 NORTH WOLLONGONG BEACH

This is a great little beach to fish just after there has been a bit of a blow from the south for tailor, Australian salmon and yellowfin bream. During the warmer months of the year you can target whiting and the odd sand flathead here with whitebait and half pilchards. You could also try using pink nippers, beach and blood worms.

5.2 SLIPPERY

This spot is very low to the water and is usually covered with a green and brown slime, so if you are going to fish from here you will need to wear the correct type of rock shoes. I would also suggest that you have your tackle and bait in a shoulder hungry bag and don't sit anything down onto the rocks as it may get washed away. Bream, luderick and silver trevally will frequent this spot.

5.3 THE WASH

I have found that this spot can really produce some good catches of bream and silver trevally on a rising and falling tide, as long as you are prepared to use berley. I find that either bread or chicken pellets

ABOVE: The northern breakwall of Wollongong Harbour can produce bream and tailor after a southerly blow.

RIGHT: Yellowtail and leatherjackets can be caught from the shore in Wollongong Harbour.

are the go. You could add a few chopped up left over pilchards. Once again you will need to fish as light as the conditions will allow. Don't fish here when there is a bit of a sea running as you will get very wet.

5.4   THE POOL

When fishing from here I prefer to fish as light as possible. All you need is a very small running ball sinker that is directly down onto the top of the bait. You will need to have a steady stream of berley to keep the bream in close to the rocks. You could always cast out a whole pilchard on a set of ganged hooks for tailor and the odd jewfish. A couple of hours either side of the high tide seems to work the best for me.

5.5   THE TAILOR HOLE

When there has been a bit of a sea running, this spot is worth casting out either a whole pilchard or garfish on a set of ganged hooks for tailor and the odd Australian salmon. Bream, drummer and silver trevally can be caught here, but you will need to have a steady berley trail. The best spots I have found while fishing here have been the end of the wall and right in adjacent to the rocks at the back of the pool. A rising tide seems to produce the better catches.

5.6   KIDDIES BEACH

Now, if you are after a place that is worth the time to bring the kids for a fish in Wollongong, this is the place to come. You may not get a lot of big fish here, but you will definitely keep the kids busy while fishing from the beach. Try using a leader of about a metre with a no. 2 ball sinker and a swivel. Blood, beach and tube worms, along with pink nippers and peeled prawns will do the trick. The kids can play in the sand while they are waiting for a bite. You could also try flicking out a few soft plastics for flathead.

5.7 THE WHARF

Another great place to bring the kids for a fish. If you don't catch any fish here you can always get the kids to chuck in some berley and watch the fish feed on the scraps. A good place to get live bait and squid. You could also try casting out a few soft plastics for flathead. Remember to retrieve them with a hopping motion and fairly slowly.

5.8 LEATHERJACKET WALL

I have caught four different species of leatherjacket from this wall. They have been the six spined, fan-tailed, yellowfin and mosaic. Try using either small pieces of peeled prawn or squid for bait and berley with chopped up prawn shells and squid.

5.9 CHRIS'S POINT

I use to bring my son here to fish for squid, leatherjackets and live yellowtail when he was young. It is a good place to bring the kids, but I would suggest that you fish as light as possible or suspend your baits under a bobby cork or small float. This place is fairly high off the water so you may want to take a long handle net with you.

5.10 SOUTH BREAKWALL

Situated on the southern side of the Wollongong boat harbour, this high, man made structure protects the fishing fleet from the prevailing north-east swells and the waves and swell that is caused by a southerly blow. Fish just on the inside of the boat harbour for luderick and leatherjackets. Excellent spot in a big sea. The front of the wall is great for tailor, bream, silver trevally, Australian salmon, pike and squid.

You could also try casting a line off the front of the wall and out to sea for drummer, groper and snapper. Try using red and green crabs for bait.

5.11 RINGBOLTS

Where the south wall of Wollongong harbour begins a very low ledge begins. It is this spot that usually has a bit of good wash running off it, but it can be very dangerous in all but very calm seas. Try berleying here for bream, drummer, leatherjackets and luderick.

It is also worth a cast with a heavy metal lure for tailor and salmon. Drummer and silver trevally can also be berleyed up here.

5.12 FLAGSTAFF POINT

Flagstaff Point is a great spot for luderick, bream, drummer, silver trevally and tailor. Try fishing the rising tide with green weed, cabbage or cunje for the drummer and luderick. Bream can't resist pink nippers, strips of mullet and striped tuna, pilly tails and blue tailed prawns. For the best results you will need to use as little lead as you can. You could always suspend your baits under a small bobby cork.

5.13 THE BOULDERS

This is one of those spots that is fairly heavily fished on the weekends, but still manages to produce very good catches of fish. I have seen other anglers wade out to the low ledge in calm seas to fish for bream, luderick and drummer, but that is not for me. I prefer to fish from the higher rocks and cast out into the deeper hole for bream, tailor, Australian salmon and the odd jewfish that can be caught here. Try using whole or half pilchards, peeled prawns and nippers for bait.

5.14 SPLASHY

It can get a bit wet when fishing from here, so I will always wear some kind of wet weather gear. Fish as light as the conditions will allow for bream, trevally, drummer and luderick on a rising and falling tide. Make sure that you have a steady berley stream going to keep the fish in the area. Cast into the washes out the back to tailor and bonito.

5.15 CAR PARK

You can either fish here off the beach or off the rocks for tailor. Australian salmon, bream and whiting. No good when the wind is coming from the south as it will blow directly onto you, but is a great spot when the seas are up a bit and the wind is coming in from the north. There is usually a bit of a rip up against the rocks that will help carry out your berley and bait to the waiting fish. You will need to also be careful of the surfers as they also use this area to get out to the breakers

Berley from this wharf for yellowtail, bream and whiting. The odd flathead and luderick can be caught here as well.

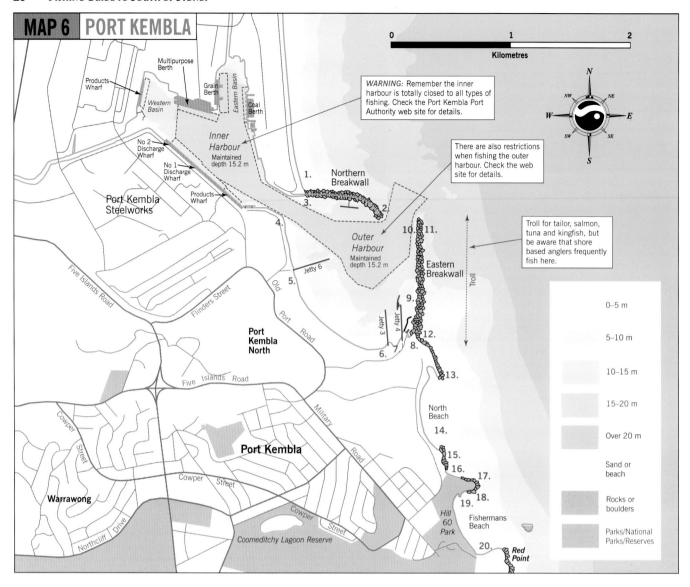

MAP 6 PORT KEMBLA

Both the Inner and Outer harbours of Port Kembla use to be accessible to anglers, but the Inner Harbour is totally closed to all types of fishing. There are also a number of restrictions when fishing the Outer Harbour so you will need to check with the local Port Authority. Nestled in the south-eastern corner is a concrete boat ramp that will give you access to the Outer Harbour and offshore.

6.1   SANDY CORNER

When the seas are too big to fish the southern break wall and the swell is wrapping around the corner of the northern break wall, this little corner is worth a shot for bream, luderick, silver trevally, tailor and Australian salmon that will feed in amongst the white water that will form up here. Fish as light as the conditions will allow you to have your bait just drifting around in the wash.

6.2   NORTHERN BREAKWALL

I have gone down to fish this break wall at times and it has been closed off to the public. This would occur when there is either work in progress on the break wall, or gas is being off loaded from a moored ship.

6.3   LEATHERJACKET LEDGE

Even though there are now a number of restrictions upon anglers when they are fishing in the Outer Harbour area you can try here for a feed of leatherjackets. I have caught six-spined, fan-belly and yellowfin leatherjackets here on a single hooked paternoster rig with a small piece of prawn or squid.

6.4   THE WALL

To gain access to this spot you will need to turn off Old Port Road an on to Christy Drive. It doesn't seem to matter whether you fish a rising or falling tide, but you will need to fish with a paternoster rig for bream and silver trevally. I have heard of a few small jewfish being caught here by those anglers who have been using fresh or live squid for bait.

6.5   MULLET WHARF

Berley up with pilchards and chicken pellets to get live mullet and yellowtail here on a rising tide. Sometimes the slimy mackerel will be so thick here you could nearly walk on the water. Fish with a small size 10 to 12 long shanked hook and a small piece of pilchard.

You may need to put a small split shot on if there is a bit of a breeze about.

6.6 AND 6.7   JETTY 3 AND JETTY 4

You cannot fish off these two jetties, but you can fish from the shore and cast out beside then for bream, silver trevally and leatherjackets. If you are fishing from a boat you will need to check with the Port Authority to how close you can go as there is a distance restriction in place.

6.8   THE BOAT RAMP

Care will need to be taken when launching and retrieving your boat when there is a swell running as there can be a bit of a surge here. This is also a great place to have a go for live bait, squid and bream, but you will need to remember not to fish directly off the ramp. There is a small break wall on the left hand side of the ramp that is a great spot when it comes to fishing for luderick. It can become much crowded when the luderick are on the chew. The odd squid and bream can be caught from here as well.

This boat ramp offers a three laned ramp with excellent amenities, including parking for about 60 cars and trailers, toilets, fish cleaning tables, boat washing area and a holding jetty.

6.9   ISLOATED BOULDER

As the name states, if you look for a rather large boulder towards the end of Jetty 4 you can fish a pair of anglers from here with a bit of room spare to put your tackle box. I like to stand here and cast out soft plastics for flathead and bream and if they are not about I will always have a squid jig handy. Just remember to keep an eye out for the coming and going of boats from the ramp in the corner. This stretch of break wall is also very good for targeting luderick and if you have a very good set of polarized sunglasses you will see them feeding along the shoreline.

6.10   THE PLATFORM

This is another place that is worth looking at, as it can hold a couple of anglers at a time to fish for bream, luderick and silver trevally on a rising or falling tide. Make sure that you have a berley trail going as you may be wasting your time. I have also caught a number of squid here.

6.11   PETE'S ROCK

The Port Authority is continually repairing and replacing the concrete blocks that form up most of this break wall. This means that you may go down one day and be able to fish off the break wall and go back a day or two later and find that it is closed whilst repair work on the wall is underway. This is a great place to target jewfish, Australian salmon, tailor, bonito, bream, drummer and the odd groper. Care needs to be taken when fishing here and it is not a place to be when the seas are big.

6.12   LIVE BAIT CORNER

Berley heavily here with chopped up pilchards and chicken pellets for yellowtail, mullet, garfish and slimy mackerel. Fish with a number 10 to 12 long hook and a very small spit shot sinker, or you could try using a small bobby cork and suspend the rig below it.

6.13   BATTERY POINT

I found this place by accident one day. When you get to the point at the northern end of the beach you will notice a rock of about three to four metres in length. If you judge the tide correctly you can stand on this rock for about an hour either side of the top of the tide and fish lightly weighted bait into the washes that are out in front of it. Once the tide has receded enough you can work your way back along the edge of the rock platform to the start of the break wall. This area is also great for those anglers who also like to fish for drummer, luderick and silver trevally. There is usually a good supply of weed and cunje on the rocks here, but you will need to get it at low tide.

6.14   NORTH BEACH

This is another place I found by accident while driving to the eastern break wall. I noticed a couple of old guys fishing off the beach for sand whiting during the month of May. They had five whiting and they had caught them on pink nippers. I have been down there a

Where the beach meets the rocks at the southern end of Battery Point is a good place to target Australian salmon and tailor.

ABOVE: Port Kembla boat ramp will give you easy access to fish the offshore reefs and islands.

RIGHT: You may not be able to fish off the wharfs any more in Port Kembla Harbour, but there are still fish to be caught while fishing just outside the gates.

BELOW: When fishing off the rocks you will need to make sure that you closely watch the waves and that you have the correct footwear on.

number of times since and also caught whiting and bream using beach, blood and tube worms.

6.15   GLOUCESTER BOULEVARD

When the swell is pumping in from the south you will usually see a number of surf board riders here. This is a good time to fish for bream and legal-sized drummer in the close washes with peeled blue-tailed prawns, nippers, cunje and strips of mullet.

6.16   SHELTERED BEACH

This small, but uninteresting beach can produces some great catches of bream and sand whiting on beach and blood worms. You could also try using pink nippers on a long leader, swivel and a number two or three bean sinker. Best fished on a falling tide and when the wind is not coming from the north.

6.17   HILL 60 NORTH

To reach this spot you will need to walk around the north side of the sewage works and fish the front ledge and washes for bream, silver trevally and drummer. When the seas are up, tailor and Australian salmon will hold up here and you may also get a number of squid. You will need to watch the waves as they can wrap around the point

High speed spinning off the southern side of Hill 60.

when the seas are up. Try using pilchards, strips of mullet, pink nippers and peeled prawns.

6.18   HILL 60 SOUTH

Access can be gained to this deep water fishing spot by walking eastward from the sewerage works cark park at the base of Hill 60. This ledge offers some great spinning for pelagics and is also a great place to bait fish for drummer, bream, silver trevally and snapper. There has also been the odd jewfish caught here over the years. There is a long, wide sunken ledge to the north of this point that makes a good spot to fish for bream and drummer in calm seas and at high tide. Just a short walk from here is an area called Pebbly Beach and it can be fished for bream, luderick, silver trevally and drummer on a falling tide. Mainly concentrate your efforts to fishing the six washes that are found here.

6.19   LENNY'S

I have managed to catch a lot of squid off the corner of this beach, but it is no good to fish when there is to much weed in the corner. Sand whiting will hold up in the corner during the summer months, but you will need to use either beach or blood worms to get them to bite. Pink nippers are also worth a try while fishing here. Not a bad spot when the winds are coming from the north.

6.20   RED POINT

The last time I went down to this place somebody had spilt red paint over the rocks, so I don't know whether it is still there, but I did manage to catch a number of bream right in the corner where the beach meets the rocks. It was a very high tide at the time and I was using beach worms and pink nippers. I was also chucking out a couple of handfuls of chicken pellets every five minutes or so.

MAP 7 LAKE ILLAWARRA

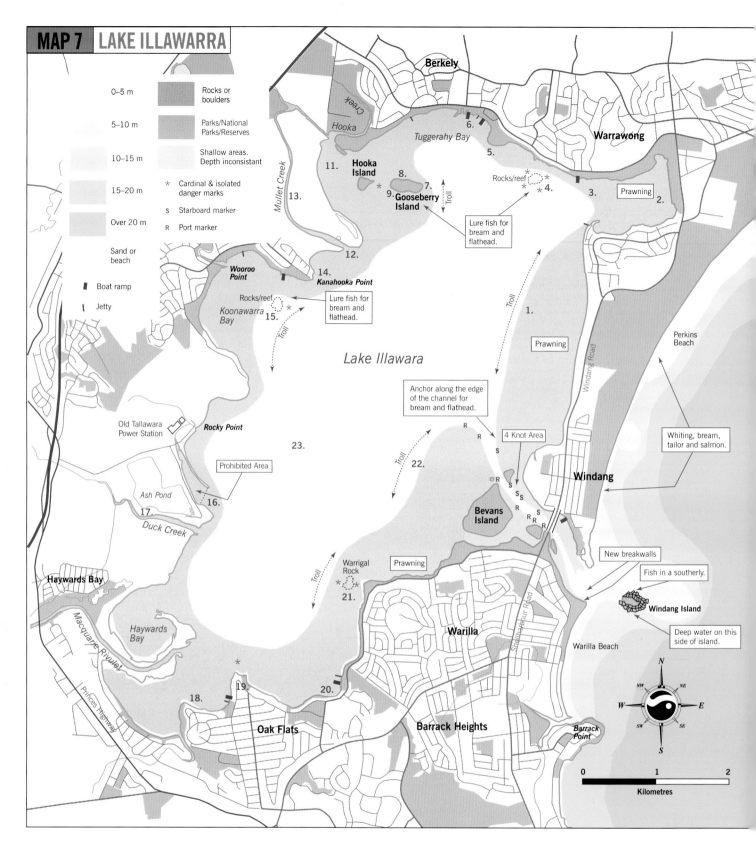

MAP 7 LAKE ILLAWARRA

When boating on this lake you will need to take care as I would class the water depth as fairly shallow. There are a number of areas that are very shallow (30cm to 50cm at high tide) and not all of these areas are clearly marked. It used to be a system that was very poorly flushed, but since the addition of two breakwalls near Windang Island the lake has had resurgence. Yellowfin bream and whiting,

dusky flathead, luderick, tailor, flounder and mullet can be caught throughout this small lake system. Australian bass can be targeted in the upper reaches of Mullet and Duck creeks. As you will see from the map there are also plenty of places to fish for the land-based angler and it is also a great lake for prawning.

Lake Illawarra is also a recreational waterway for the Illawarra

Region for sailing, water skiing and canoeing. Hooka and Gooseberry islands in the northern area of the lake comprise the Berkeley Reserve.

January in the 'gong always produces great fishing as the summer season really kicks into gear. Whether it's because everyone is relaxed and taking in the warm days and sunshine or most people are on holidays, there seem to be fish being caught everywhere. Lake Illawarra will always have a bit of added fishing pressure applied to it whenever holiday makers descend on the numerous caravan parks around the lake foreshores.

7.1 TROLLING RUN 1

This stretch of shoreline is fairly shallow and weedy, but if you like trolling for dusky flathead, bream and the odd tailor you will need to work the area where the weed beds meet the sand and the drop-off. When trolling here you will need to troll as slow as you possibly can, just above idle would be fine. If you have a large motor I would suggest that you cut a small hole in the bottom of a bucket and tie it off the front of your boat. This will definitely slow the speed down. This same set of weed beds is a great place to catch garfish, mullet and prawns

7.2 GRIFFINS BAY

Not a lot happens in this small and very shallow bay. That is except when the prawns are running during the dark of the moon during the summer months. It is usually at this time of the year that the shoreline and shallower areas light up with anglers who are out trying to get a feed of prawns.

7.3 BAMES PARK

There is a small wharf beside the boat ramp in Bames Park that is worth a shot for mullet and garfish. You can also target leatherjackets, bream and dusky flathead here on a rising tide. Due to the fact that there is a fair amount of weed on the bottom you could try suspending a live poddy mullet or prawn under a float. Surface lures for bream and flathead are also worth a shot. Great place to bring the kids for a fish.

7.4 TOM'S REEF

This area is a great place to try out those surface poppers and lures for bream, whiting and dusky flathead in the early hours and just

Dusky flathead are suckers for those bladed lures when worked along any of the edges of weedbeds and drop offs that can be found in Lake Illawarra.

The author with a beautiful dusky flathead. Lake Illawarra is renowned for them during the summer months.

before the sun sets. You could also try anchoring here and laying out a fine berley trail for mullet, garfish, pike, whiting, bream and leatherjackets. Try using a long leader rig when fishing beside the reef and very little lead when fishing on top of the reef. Luderick are also caught here on a rising and falling tide.

7.5 WOLLAMAI POINT

Access to this shallow and patchy point can be gained by walking along the bike track from Wollamai. Best fished here on a rising tide and early in the morning during the summer months for bream and dusky flathead with either soft plastic or surface poppers. Cast towards the areas that have patches of sand and rocks for the best results.

7.6 BERKELEY HARBOUR

The Berkeley Harbour ramp will give you a safe and easy access to all of Lake Illawarra. You can fish off the shore from here, but I would suggest that you try fishing during the week. I have been out in my boat and cast hard bodied lures and soft plastics back to the break wall that protects this small harbour for bream, whiting, luderick and flathead.

7.7 DROP-OFF

I have had my best results fishing here when the tide is falling. You can either anchor at the edge of the drop-off, berley and feed out lightly weighted baits for whiting, bream, flathead, tailor and the odd luderick. If bait fishing is not your scene you can try working this whole area with soft plastics and metal vibes in the deeper water or hard bodied lures in the shallow areas near the shoreline.

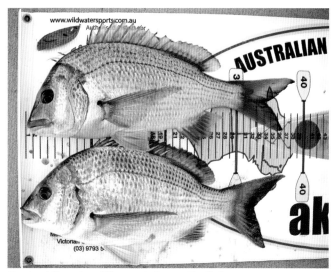

Check out the colour difference in these yellowfin bream.

7.8 OYSTER REEF

Work this whole northern face of the island for bream, flathead, whiting, pike and long toms. Very shallow with reef, oystered cover fingers and weed beds throughout its entire length.

7.9 WEED BEDS

Bream, whiting, dusky flathead and mullet will feed over this set of weed beds during the last two hours of the run-up and the first two hours of the run-out tides. Surface lures, poppers and lightly weighted soft plastics are the go here. The bite will vary here when carrying out this type of fishing, especially for the bream. Sometimes the bream will smash the lure and at other times they will just play with it

7.10 HOOKA CREEK

During the many times that I have fished in this small creek I have yet to see a bait angler. It has always been someone flicking out hard bodied lures or soft plastics for bream and flathead. You can also catch luderick and whiting in this creek. The occasional Australian bass has been caught in this small creek in the deeper holes, snags and rock bars.

7.11 KOONG-BURRY BAY

This bay is best fished a couple of hours either side of the high tide. The whole area is a combination of weed beds with small patches of sand dotted in between. There can also be a number of logs and dead tress found in this bay. Bream, flathead, whiting, luderick and mullet are the main fish species caught here

7.12 MULLET CREEK ENTRANCE

I haven't done a lot of fishing here, but I have been told that it is best fished on a run-out tide. Anchor close to the shore on either side of the entrance, berley with chopped up pilchards and chicken pellets for bream and flathead. During the winter months you can target luderick as well.

7.13 MULLET CREEK

Now this creek goes up a fair way and can be fished from both the boat and the shoreline. Bream, mullet, luderick, flathead, garfish, tailor and Australian bass can be caught in this creek. A couple of years ago I was fishing under the highway bridge in a boat and came across a school of bream feeding just below the surface and no matter what type of lure or soft plastic I cast towards them they were not interested, but when the sun went off the water they started to smash surface poppers and soft plastics.

7.14 KANAHOOKA POINT

There is a small boat ramp situated on the point here that will give you access to the lake and Mullet Creek. You can fish from the shore for mullet, garfish, bream and the odd flathead or two. Can be very weedy at times.

7.15 MANNS REEF

This reef is similar to Tom's Reef and can be fished the same way. This area is a great place to try out those surface poppers and lures for bream, whiting and dusky flathead in the early hours and just before the sun sets. You could also try anchoring and laying out a fine berley trail for mullet, garfish, pike, whiting, bream and leatherjackets. Try using a long leader rig when fishing beside the reef and very little lead when fishing on top of the reef. Luderick are also caught here on a rising and falling tide.

7.16 TALLAWARRA STEEL GRIDS

You can actually drive right up to the steel grills and look through them to see bream milling on the other side. However, trying to catch them is another thing. I usually work the front of the grills by slowly drifting parallel and casting a soft plastic towards the shore. When you do hook up, it could be all over in a milli-second as they take off for the grills.

7.17 DUCK CREEK

This is the smallest of the three main creeks that feed into Lake Illawarra. It does produce the odd catch of flathead, bream, mullet and garfish on the run-out tide.

7.18 AND 7.19 KURRURA TO YANGAR POINT

There is a boat ramp situated in between these two points which will give you easy access to the southern section of the lake where you can target bream, mullet and garfish with bait and dusky flathead with either live poddy mullet or soft plastics. You could also try trolling at a slow speed for flathead and tailor. The odd pike and long tom can be caught as well.

7.20 DAVIES BAY

There is another small boat ramp here that will also give you access to the southern side of the lake. You can fish from the shore for bream, mullet and garfish. Make sure that you use berley.

7.21 WARRIGAL ROCKS

This area is very similar to Tom's Reef in the northern half of the lake and is another great place to try out those surface poppers and lures for bream, whiting and dusky flathead in the early hours and just before sunset. You could also try anchoring here and laying out a fine berley trail for mullet, garfish, pike, whiting, bream and leatherjackets. Try using a long leader rig when fishing beside the reef and very little lead when fishing on top of the reef. Luderick are also caught on a rising and falling tide.

7.22 TROLLING RUN 2

As with Trolling Run 1, this stretch of shoreline is fairly shallow and weedy, but if you like trolling for dusky flathead, bream and the odd tailor, work the area where the weed beds meet the sand and the drop-off. When trolling here, you will need to travel as slowly as you possibly can, just above idle would be fine. With a large motor, you can cut a small hole in the bottom of a bucket and tie it off the front of your boat which will definitely slow the speed down. This same set of weed beds is a great place to catch garfish, mullet and prawns.

7.23 THE WEED BEDS

You will need to take care whilst travelling across this area as it is not clearly sign posted. There are plenty of shallow areas here that have a combination of sand and weed patches. Bream, whiting, flathead, mullet and garfish are regularly caught off these weed beds.

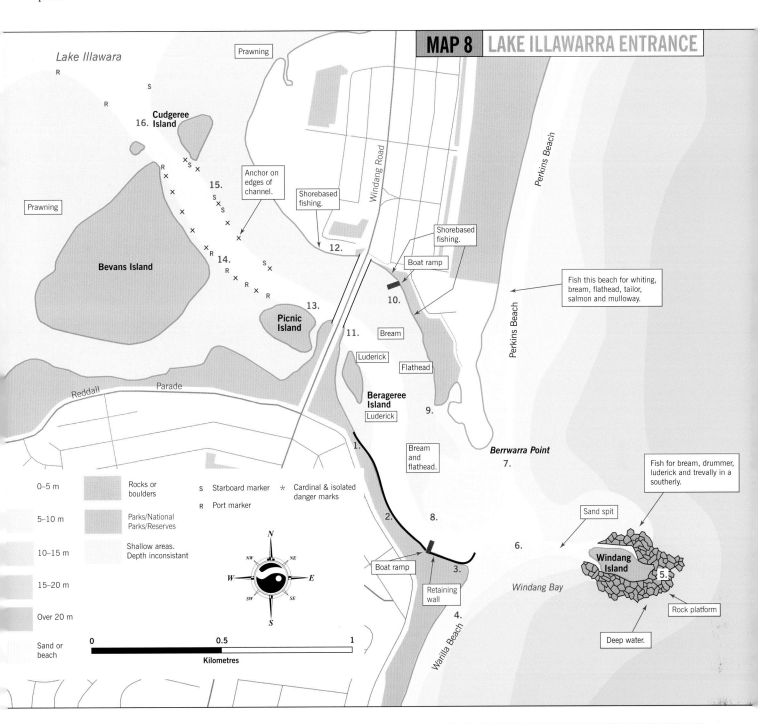

MAP 8 LAKE ILLAWARRA ENTRANCE

The opening of the entrance to Lake Illawarra now provides an abundance of fresh prawns in season, and fish all year round. The lake also provides an excellent venue for various water sports including sailing, skiing and windsurfing. There are many locations around the foreshores of the lake where access to the water is available.

One of the most popular fishing spots is the mouth of Lake Illawarra, a shallow lagoon of some 33 square kilometres. The inlet is located a few kilometres north of Shellharbour at Warilla (a rearrangement of three of the four syllables of 'Illawarra'). Here, virtually 24 hours a day, fishermen can be seen dangling their lines from the Windang Bridge.

ABOVE: These anglers were targeting mullet and garfish off the end of this small breakwall.

BELOW: This pelicon was keeping an eye out for a free feed from anglers who were targeting luderick.

8.1 REDDALL RESERVE

This is a great shore-based spot that has plenty of nearby parking. From here you can fish for bream, sand whiting, dusky flathead and tailor. For those of you that prefer to use hard body lures and soft plastics you can try working them from the deeper water and back up onto the shallows. I have found that berleying is a must when fishing here. Make up your berley in a bucket and every five minutes throw out a handful. This will usually keep the fish in the area. Also the shallow water closest to the bridge is a great place to prawn during the summer months.

8.2 THE HUT

Sand whiting and the odd bream are caught from here. Fishing from beside the boat ramp is a good place to start as the returning anglers will usually clean their catch here and this makes a great berley. Fish as light as the conditions will allow. You could also try using a small stemmed cork float here with live poddy mullet.

8.3 WHITING CORNER

As the name suggest, this area is a great place to target sand whiting during the summer months and bream during the winter months. The best time to fish here is during the run-out tide. Try using squirt, blood and beach worms for bait. You could also give live pink nippers ago as well. The odd large dusky flathead has been caught here over the years.

8.4 WARILLA BEACH

During the summer months you can catch sand whiting, yellowfin bream and mulloway here. Best times to target them are when the light is at its lowest or when you have an overcast day. Half a pilchard, beach and blood worms and pink nippers are the gun baits for the whiting and bream, while live and stripped mullet, strips and whole squid and whole pilchards are the go for the mulloway. Try working the edges deep gutters and the sand banks during the run-up tide. Once the tide has turned, position your baits in the deeper area off the beach.

8.5 WINDANG ISLAND

As with all rock fishing care needs to be taken when fishing off any rock platform. Once you have crossed the sand spit you will find a small gutter on the northern side of the island. Try here for bream and whiting. Half way along this northern face you will come to a section of the platform that is a little bit higher than the rest. It is here you can cast lightly weighted bait for bream and drummer. No good to fish here during a northerly swell.

The front of the island drops away into deep water where there are drummer, bream, snapper, luderick and squid. For the high speeding spinning angler you can also target Australian salmon, tailor, bonito, kingfish and tuna. The southern side of the island is worth a shot for bream and drummer when the seas are up a little bit, but care will still need to be taken when fishing here. It is also a place where you can catch your live bait.

8.6 THE SAND SPIT

Target whiting and bream on a rising tide with beach and blood worms. You could also try using live pink nippers. This is a good place to cast out a slab of fresh mullet, luderick or tailor during the night for a mulloway.

8.7 PERKINS BEACH

When fishing here you would fish it the same as you would Warrilla Beach. During the summer months you can catch sand whiting, yellowfin bream and mulloway here. Best times to target them are when the light is at its lowest or when you have an overcast day. Half a pilchard, beach and blood worms and pink nippers are the gun baits for the whiting and bream, while live and stripped mullet, strips and whole squid and whole pilchards are the go for the mulloway. Try working the edges, deep gutters and the sand banks during the run-up tide. Once the tide has turned, position your baits in the deeper area off the beach.

8.8 THE CORNER

It doesn't seem to matter when you fish here for sand whiting, as long as there is some run in the water. You could also try fishing for yellowfin bream with a long leader and pink nippers for bait. Dusky flathead can be targeted here with soft plastics on the run-out tide.

8.9 PINE TREE PARK

Anchor near the edge of the weed beds that are located here for luderick. Local green weed and squirt worms are the go. When it is calm I prefer to use a pencil or quill float and when there is a bit of a breeze up I will up grade to a stemmed cork float, as this will make it easier to see. You could also work the edge of the weed beds with an electric motor and soft plastics

The new breakwall to the entrance of Lake Illawarra has made a great deal of difference to the fishing in the lake and the beaches either side of the entrance.

for bream and dusky flathead. During the summer months you can go prawning in the shallow parts near the shoreline.

8.10 MOORINGS

Bream, dusky flathead and luderick will feed in and around the moored boats. Anchor up current of them and lay out a slow, but small berley trail to attract the fish out from under the boats. You will need to have a leader length of between one to two metres in length, a swivel and a size 1 to 2 ball sinker. This will allow the bait to move around in the current while the sinker is anchored on the bottom.

8.11 LUDERICK ALLEY

Luderick can be seen feeding along the edges of the weed beds too, but you will need fresh weed and berley. A few flounder are about taking baits meant for flathead, while there are some small leatherjackets along the rock walls and chopper tailor in the main basin. Using fresh cabbage weed from the rocks, and fishing the white water should produce a few fish.

8.12 THE BOAT SHED

Some quality whiting can be caught out in front of the boat shed and to have a good chance of getting amongst a few you will need to get yourself a few squirt worms. Don't be surprised if you hook a couple of big blackfish on the worms either, they readily snap up squirt worms throughout the year. The worms can be obtained by using a nipper pump over the shallow sand flats at low tide. Just look for the small holes in the sand and pump away. Luderick can also be seen feeding along the edges of the weed beds too, but you will need fresh weed and berley.

8.13 PICNIC ISLAND

If there is a bit of wind blow from the north while you are fishing here, you will need to use two anchors. This will allow you to fish parallel to the bank as the tide either moves in or out. Fish for luderick, sand whiting, bream and flathead. You could also drift along this stretch of bank and cast out a few lures or soft plastics for bream and dusky flathead.

8.14   THE DEEP HOLE

Due to the fact that the tide can run a bit fast at this spot, it has scoured out a deep hole in the corner of the island. Dusky flathead, bream and whiting can be caught here using bait, soft plastics and lures. Try small poddy mullet, garfish and pink nippers for bait.

8.15   JUDBOWLEY POINT

Access can be gained here to a great land-based spot for bream, flathead, whiting, garfish and luderick by parking in Judbowley

Parade. It can become very crowded on the weekends, so I would try and fish here either early in the morning or later in the afternoon. It can be a bit snaggy here at times, so try using a paternoster rig.

8.16   THE PASSAGE

This stretch of water narrows off as it leads into the lake proper. You can either anchor or drift here for flounder, flathead, whiting and bream. Care needs to be taken when anchoring as you should leave enough room for the travelling boats.

MAP 9 WARRILLA BEACH TO SHELLHARBOUR

Shellharbour is a charming township on the coast and is one of the oldest settlements in NSW. It is situated 25 km from Central Wollongong and 106 km south of Sydney. Inevitably in recent times it has become a bedroom suburb as Greater Wollongong has spread south. Now it has a small shopping centre, a pub, a post office, and a few services.

Shellharbour has rewarding fishing, brilliant beaches, saltwater pools, clubs, terrific night life and great accommodation. There are also a number of excellent cycle ways that are perfect for either riding a bike or just going for a walk.

Shell Harbour is normally used as a jumping off point for those anglers who are going to fish offshore, but the harbour itself can put on some great fishing at times, especially during and after a big sea.

The haven is a great place to fish when seas are up. White water will push into the haven and provide cover for the fish.

9.1   WARRILLA BEACH

Warrilla beach fishes extremely well if the lake is flowing out south of Windang Island. The target fish here are bream, whiting, tailor and jewfish. The run-out seems to produce the better catches, especially if it is either early in the morning or late in the afternoon. Try fishing the edges of the deeper gutters and if there is a bit of a rip working, try using the pull of the rip to take your larger baits out for the jewfish.

9.2 AND 9.3   BARRACK POINT

There are a number of spots on this small, but very productive headland that produce bream, drummer, luderick, tailor, Australian salmon and the odd kingfish or two. A cast of about 50 metres will

South Shellharbour beach and rocks can produce bream, silver trevally and luderick on a rising tide.

get you out onto the sandy/gravel bottom that is found around this headland to catch snapper and jewfish.

9.4   BARRACK HEIGHTS

It is worth a shot for bream and whiting off the end of the beach here on a rising tide. Better if you can time your fishing outing to about a couple of hours before the sun sets. Pink nippers, beach and blood worms are the go for bait. To get the best results you will need to berley and fish as light as possible.

9.5   BARDSLEY PARK

Not the best beach corner to fish from in a northerly wind, but can be successfully fished when the wind is coming from the south. Especially after there has been a bit of a blow. Bream, drummer and the odd whiting can be caught here on a rising tide.

9.6   SHELL HARBOUR POINT

This rock shelf is located directly in front of the caravan park and while it's not a good day spot, it excels during the low light periods and at night. The point consists of flat sandstone and is criss-crossed with a number of sandy/gravel gutters, holes and crevices. A great place to fish for bream, drummer and luderick while using pink nippers, peeled prawns and fresh squid as bait.

9.7   SHELL HARBOUR BOAT HAVEN

Fish amongst the moorings for yellowtail and bream. The small break wall will produce good catches of bream, drummer and luderick during big seas. When it is too rough to fish off the breakwalls you could always try fishing off the boat ramp and the loading wharf, as the swell surges up and down the ramp for bream, silver trevally and luderick.

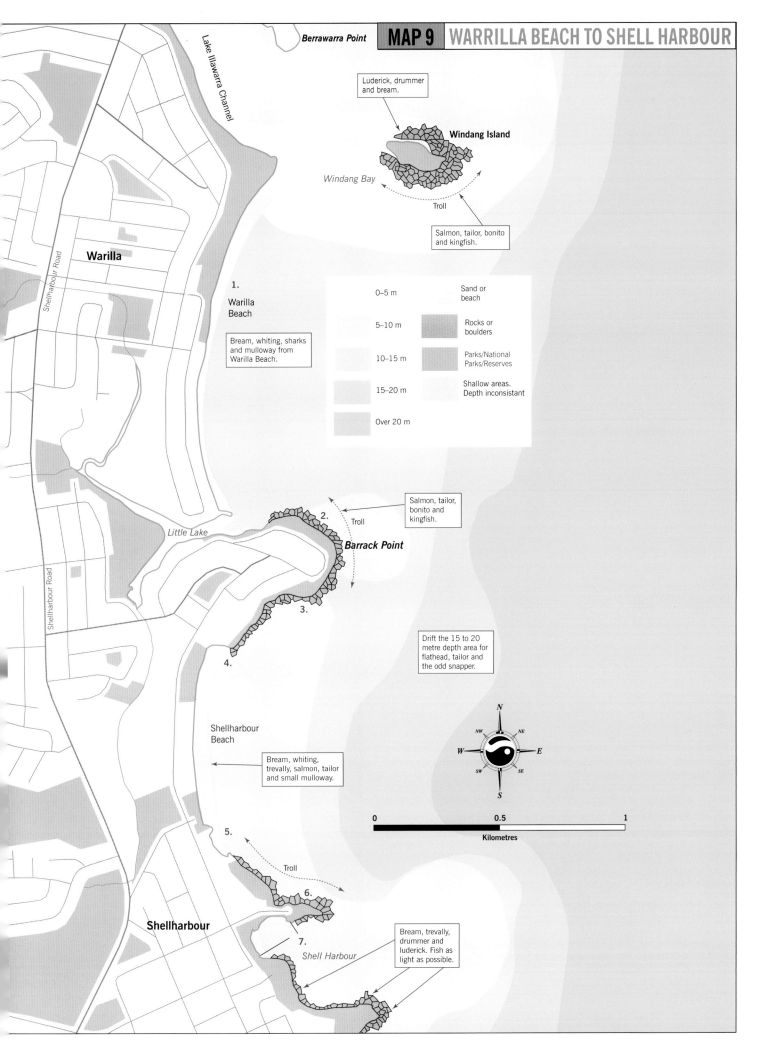

Luderick, drummer and bream.

Windang Island

Windang Bay

Troll

Salmon, tailor, bonito and kingfish.

Warilla

1.

Warilla Beach

Bream, whiting, sharks and mulloway from Warilla Beach.

0–5 m		Sand or beach
5–10 m		Rocks or boulders
10–15 m		Parks/National Parks/Reserves
15–20 m		Shallow areas. Depth inconsistant
Over 20 m		

Little Lake

2.

Troll

Barrack Point

Salmon, tailor, bonito and kingfish.

3.

4.

Drift the 15 to 20 metre depth area for flathead, tailor and the odd snapper.

Shellharbour Beach

Bream, whiting, trevally, salmon, tailor and small mulloway.

N
NW   NE
W   E
SW   SE
S

0   0.5   1
Kilometres

5.

Troll

6.

Shellharbour

7.

Bream, trevally, drummer and luderick. Fish as light as possible.

Shell Harbour

Lake Illawarra Channel

Shellharbour Road

Shellharbour Road

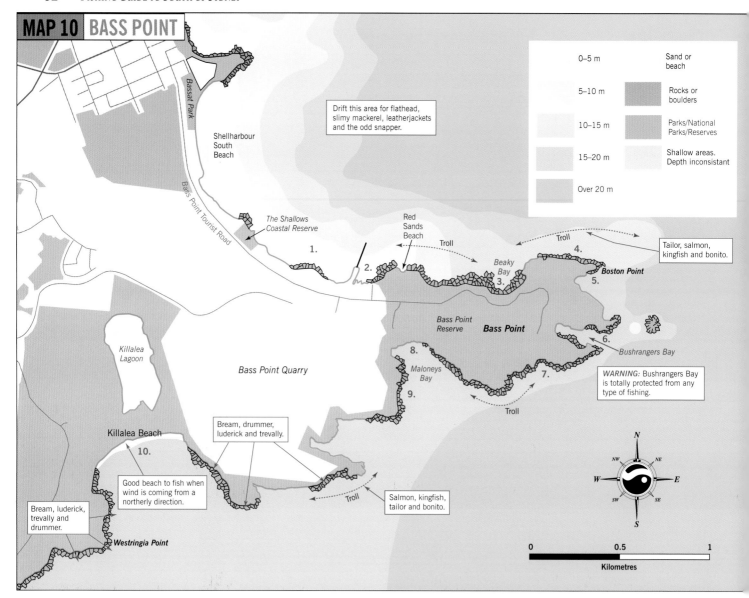

MAP 10 BASS POINT

Drift this area for flathead, slimy mackerel, leatherjackets and the odd snapper.

Tailor, salmon, kingfish and bonito.

WARNING: Bushrangers Bay is totally protected from any type of fishing.

Bream, drummer, luderick and trevally.

Good beach to fish when wind is coming from a northerly direction.

Bream, luderick, trevally and drummer.

Salmon, kingfish, tailor and bonito.

0–5 m

5–10 m

10–15 m

15–20 m

Over 20 m

Sand or beach

Rocks or boulders

Parks/National Parks/Reserves

Shallow areas. Depth inconsistant

MAP 10 BASS POINT

The Bass Point area is just south of Shellharbour and is one of the most prolific fishing spots on the near south coast. This rock finger of land that juts out into the passing currents is a natural gathering ground for many different species. Snapper, bream, drummer, tailor, Australian salmon, pike, silver trevally, kingfish, bonito and groper, to name a few.

Baits like cunjevoi, crabs, green weed and cabbage can be gathered, but you will need to check the NSW Fisheries regulations as there are a couple of restrictions when fishing here. On the north-eastern shore of Bass Point a car park allows good access to rocky gutters, sand and weedy bottoms and a few small bomboras and washes. There are also a number of walking tracks, barbeque areas, picnic spots and camping areas.

10.1   RED SANDS

During my earlier years I used to do a lot of surfing and when the swell was up and the conditions were right I would surf here or on the reef on the other side of the blue metal loader. It was also during conditions like those that I caught many bream, drummer and groper from this area, but you need to watch out for breaking waves.

The author with a pair of thumping drummer.

The Blue Metal loader can be fished from a boat or off the shore.

10.2   BLUE METAL LOADER

Nestled in the corner here is a very small boat ramp that can give you access to offshore fishing. However, you will need to take care if launching when there is a swell running as the water surges up and down the ramp. This is not such a bad place to go and get some of your live bait as squid, yellowtail, mullet and garfish can be berleyed up here at times. When the big seas are running and the swell is either coming straight into this small bay or wrapping around the point, you can fish this area for bream, snapper, silver trevally, the odd tailor and Australian salmon.

10.3   BEAKY BAY

This small bay does produce the odd bream and drummer, but I have found this small bay good to target squid, yellowtail and sea garfish. Just after there has been a bit of a blow, I have seen a couple of anglers fish this area for snapper and jewfish, but you would need to get a decent cast in to reach the sandy/ gravel areas.

10.4   THE NORTHERN POINT

You will find cunje, cabbage and weed growing off this side of the point. This will in turn attract bream, drummer, luderick and silver trevally. Early morning and late in the afternoon is worth a shot by casting out a few metal slicers or large soft plastic stick baits for tailor, Australian salmon and the odd kingfish and bonito.

10.5   INSIDE COVE

This large and deep cove can be reached by walking east from the car park for about 750 metres and it produces silver trevally, drummer, bream, Australian salmon, tailor, pike, luderick and groper. I have found the best time to fish here is about an hour and a half before the top of the tide and about two hours of the falling tide. Fish as light as possible with a small ball sinker that sits directly on top of the bait. Try using peeled prawns, pink nipper, half pillies and strips of mullet and tuna for bait. Green weed, cabbage and cunje will do for the luderick and drummer.

10.6   BUSHRANGERS BAY –
SANCTUARY ZONE

Bushrangers Bay may look like a very inviting place to fish, but it is an aquatic reserve nursery for juvenile fish species and other marine life, and is totally protected.

10.7   DEEP POINT

You can fish off the southern side of Bushrangers Bay towards the south for Australian salmon and tailor. It is quite high and safe here in most seas. This southern side is also a great place to suspend live bait out under a bobby cork for kingfish and tuna. If you try using cuttlefish or squid for bait you will also have a chance of getting a snapper or two. Especially on a rising tide.

10.8 AND 10.9 MALONEYS BAY

Access to Maloney's Bay can be by parking in the car park and working your way down to the water level. The bay can produce good catches of bream, drummer and silver trevally on a rising tide if the swell is coming from the north. The white water area that is found in this bay will also produce tailor, salmon and bonito. Try using either a whole garfish or pilchard on a set of ganged hooks.

10.10 KILLALEA BEACH (THE FARM)

This is another place where I used to surf when I was younger, especially when the swell was coming from the south and the winds were coming from the north. Not only does this beach produce great surfing conditions, at times it is a great place to fish for bream and whiting with either beach or blood worms.

ABOVE: Tailor love feeding in and around the washes that are found off the end of Bass Point.

BELOW: Target bream, drummer and groper at Red Sands.

BOAT RAMPS Wollongong—Stanwell Park Beach to Bass Point

Name	Make	Condition	No of Lanes	Wash Down	Lights	Fish Clean	BBQ	Toilets
Map 1 Stanwell Park Beach to Coalcliff Point								
Headlands Drive Austinmer	Beach sand	Poor	1	No	Yes	No	Yes	Yes
Map 4 Bellambi Point								
Robert Cram Drive Bellambi beach	Concrete	Excel	4	Yes	Yes	Yes	Yes	No
Map 5 Wollongong Harbour								
Wollongong Harbour	Concrete	Good	1	Yes	Yes	No	No	Yes
Map 6 Port Kembla								
Foreshore Road Port Kembla	Concrete	Excellent	3	Yes	Yes	Yes	No	Yes
Map 7 Lake Illawarra								
Berkeley Northcliffe Drive Lake Illawarra	Concrete	Good	2	No	No	No	No	Yes
Berkeley Northcliffe Drive Berkeley Harbour Lake Illawarra	Concrete	Good	2	No	Yes	No	No	Yes
Berkeley Northcliffe Drive Illawarra Yacht Club	Concrete	Good	2	Yes	Yes	Yes	No	No
Kanahooka Drive Berkeley	Concrete	Good	2	Yes	Yes	No	No	Yes
Oak Flats Sailing Club The Boulevarde Oak Flats	Concrete	Good	1	Yes	Yes	No	Yes	Yes
Oak Flats Ski Park The Esplanade Oak Flats	Concrete	Good	1	Yes	Yes	No	Yes	Yes
Map 8 Lake Illawarra Entrance								
Reddel Parade Lake Illawarra	Concrete	Good	1	No	Yes	No	Yes	Yes
Fern Street near Windang Bridge	Concrete	Good	2	Yes	Yes	Yes	Yes	Yes
Map 9 Windang Island to Barrack Point to Shellharbour								
Towns Street Shellharbour	Concrete	Good	2	Yes	Yes	Yes	Yes	Yes
Map 10 Bass Point								
Bass Point Tourist Road Bass Point	Concrete	Good	2	No	No	No	No	No

TACKLE SHOPS Wollongong—Stanwell Park Beach to Bass Point

LEISURE COAST BAIT AND TACKLE
279 Rothery Rd Corrimal
PHONE: (02) 4284 2734

FERGO'S TACKLE WORLD WOLLONGONG
4/135 Princess Highway Fairy Meadow, NSW 2519
PHONE: (02) 4225 7233

DAPTO BAIT AND TACKLE
92 Lakeside Drive Koonawarra
PHONE: (02)4261 3322

HELLRAISER TACKLE
243 Princes Highway Albion Park
PHONE: (02) 4256 6600

THE TACKLE SHOP
632 Addison St Shellharbour
PHONE: (02) 4295 3999

DEAN'S TACKLE AND OUTDOORS
312 Windang Rd Windang
PHONE: (02) 4295 1615

WINDANG BAIT AND TACKLE
237 Windang Rd Windang
PHONE: (02) 4297 6511

CHAPTER 2
KIAMA
Minnamurra Point to Seven Mile Beach at Gerroa

The pelicans are on fish watch at the Kiama Harbour boat ramp.

The town of Kiama is famous for the Blowhole that was first visited by George Bass in 1797. To view the Blowhole when it is working, you will need to time your visit when the seas are running from the south-east and the swell reasonably large. Kiama also has the Little Blowhole, Black Beach and Cathedral Rocks. All of these craggy headlands and sheltered coves rest against a backdrop of fertile farming land. Many of the buildings in the Kiama area are heritage listed, too, and are well worth a visit from the avid history buff.

Other places that are also worth a visit when the fish are not on the chew are Jamberoo Valley (for its pub, recreation area and general rural attractions), the lush Minnamurra Rainforest, Minnamurra Falls and the Barren Grounds nature reserve, set high on the escarpment behind Kiama.

Heading south along the Princes Highway from Kiama and passing through the postcard-perfect Kiama bends, you really need to detour off this artery toward the east and take in the magnificent beaches and sleepy villages of Werri Beach, Gerringong and Gerroa. I lived in Gerroa for 16 years and have regularly visited the place ever since. It has grown in that time, but hasn't lost its seaside village character.

Fishing in and around Kiama is very enjoyable, productive and quite popular. There are many forms of fishing that can be done in and around the Kiama district; from freshwater to deep sea. The region offers some great rock fishing, game and reef fishing, beach and river fishing and bass fishing in the upper reaches of the various rivers and creeks.

Kiama is especially popular as a land-based rock fishing destination — particularly from Kiama's striking Blowhole Point rocks. Here you can catch a wide range of fish species. In the summer months it is common for many people to try their luck at live baiting for passing game fish such as black marlin, various tuna, kingfish, sharks, the odd wayward cobia and much more. Also popular is spinning with metal fishing lures, such as Raiders and Halcos. You can often spin up yellowtail kingfish, mackerel tuna (kawa-kawa), bonito, tailor, Australian salmon, frigate mackerel, pike and more here.

On the southern side of the Blowhole Point, squid are sometimes plentiful and you can catch very good numbers at times for either bait or to eat, but please take only what you need and can use. Using a prawn-style squid jig ('jag') or squid pole and natural bait will definitely do the trick when it comes to catching some of these tasty ten-armed guys.

Kiama Blowhole is not the only popular rock fishing spot in this area. Other venues that also produce quite well are the southern rock point of Surf Beach, especially for salmon and tailor. The stretch of coast between the northern end of East's Beach and the Little Blowhole Point (Marsdens Headland) is also great for many fish species, including some quite reasonable snapper at times (mostly after a spell of heavy swell).

MAP 11 MINNAMURRA POINT TO BOMBO BEACH

The Bombo Headland has an extraordinary geological feature, clusters of hexagonal basalt columns are an internationally recognised phenomena. The Headland can be accessed via the Kiama Walking Trail, which starts near the Kiama Golf Course.

A legacy of blue metal quarrying in the 1880s has left a moonscape of basalt walls and columns. A regular backdrop to video clips eg Power Rangers and television commercials; it is located at the northern end of Bombo Beach or accessed from the Cliff Drive cycleway.

Use Northern or Southern Bombo exits to access Riverside Dve, then North Kiama Dve, then Cliff Drive.

Fishing from Bombo beach can produce whiting, dart, bream and flathead off the sand. Whilst off the rock points you will find bream, silver trevally, Australian salmon and tailor using pilchards and strip baits.

11.1 MINNAMURRA POINT

This small, but very productive headland is well worth a spot of fishing for bream, tailor, silver trevally, whiting, luderick and drummer in the washes and gutters that are found here. This area can be a bit on the snaggy side, so you will need to fish as light as the conditions will allow.

11.2 MINNAMURRA BEACH

Minnamurra Beach or 'Mystics', a favourite with the locals, is a very popular surfing spot just off the Minnamurra River estuary. It is part of the 250 hectares of pristine coastal reserve sited on 8 km of coastline and has one of the best surf beaches on the south coast of New South Wales. This natural setting features small areas of vegetation with a view out to stunning Stack Island.

Day visits are very popular, people coming for the scenery, the surfing, for barbecues and picnics at nearby Minnamurra River Reserve with access off Charles Avenue, Minnamurra. Bream, tailor, whiting and flathead can be caught off the beach.

11.3 BONEYARD

For those of you that still surf and fish, the Boneyard has the best of both worlds. When the seas are coming from a northerly direction and the winds are coming from the south, the Boneyard can turn on great surf. Now if the swell and wind are coming from the south this small bay and headland is very popular for bream, silver trevally, drummer and groper in and around the base of the headlands. Tailor, Australian salmon, bonito, tuna and kingfish can be caught here by high speed spinning and live baiting.

Another really interesting aspect of the Boneyard is the exceptional fishing it can offer after prolonged spells of very rough seas. Following at least three or four days of destructive storm surge (ideally accompanied by heavy rain), the sheltered waters of the bay attract vast numbers of luderick

When you go for a walk around the rocks north of Bombo Beach you will come across a number of great washes that will hold Australian salmon like this one.

You can work the washes on Bombo Headland for snapper just as the sun either rises or sets.

(blackfish) as well as a few bream, drummer and even the odd mulloway or jewfish. The prolific and hungry blackfish are best pursued using a paternoster rig with one or two No. 4 hooks on short droppers, baited with smelly meat cut from the "lazy man's cunjevoi" that washes up in huge clumps along the back of the bay and adjoining beaches in such conditions. Storms of this severe magnitude usually only occur once or twice each year at most, but when they do, switched-on anglers descend upon the Boneyard 'en masse' for some truly memorable fishing action!

11.4 NORTH BOMBO HEADLAND

Access can be gained by walking from the car park at the northern end of Bombo Beach. The southern side of the headland is worth a shot for bream, luderick, silver trevally, tailor and Australian salmon. As you work you way around the headland the water will deepen and you can fish for the above fish species as well as snapper, kingfish and other pelagics. Care needs to be taken when fishing here.

The front of the headland has a few gutters that are worth fishing in for drummer, luderick and bream on a rising tide.

11.5 BOMBO BEACH

Bombo can be a very treacherous beach to swim from as it has a forever-changing beach and gutters. It is these formations that provide good fishing. Parking is available at both the southern and northern ends of the beach. Salmon and tailor are prolific during the winter months, especially at dawn and dusk. Pilchards on gang hooks are probably the best bait to use. Summer produces bream, whiting and flathead. Bream are more prevalent towards both the north and south ends of the beach near the rocky points. Mulloway can be found most of the year at night. You can also try beach worming towards the middle of the beach where it is usually a bit flatter.

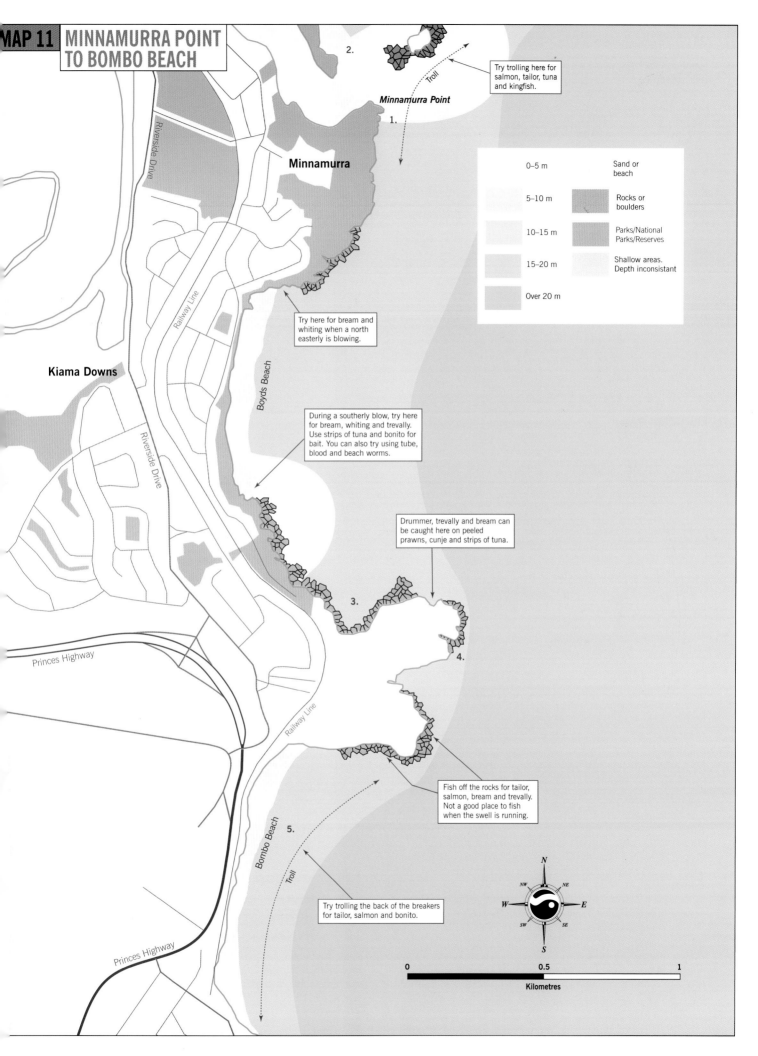

MAP 11 MINNAMURRA POINT TO BOMBO BEACH

2.

Try trolling here for salmon, tailor, tuna and kingfish.

Minnamurra Point

Troll

1.

Minnamurra

0–5 m | Sand or beach

5–10 m | Rocks or boulders

10–15 m | Parks/National Parks/Reserves

15–20 m | Shallow areas. Depth inconsistant

Over 20 m

Riverside Drive

Railway Line

Kiama Downs

Try here for bream and whiting when a north easterly is blowing.

Boyds Beach

During a southerly blow, try here for bream, whiting and trevally. Use strips of tuna and bonito for bait. You can also try using tube, blood and beach worms.

Riverside Drive

Drummer, trevally and bream can be caught here on peeled prawns, cunje and strips of tuna.

3.

4.

Princes Highway

Railway Line

Fish off the rocks for tailor, salmon, bream and trevally. Not a good place to fish when the swell is running.

Bombo Beach

5.

Troll

Try trolling the back of the breakers for tailor, salmon and bonito.

N
NW | NE
W | E
SW | SE
S

Princes Highway

0   0.5   1

Kilometres

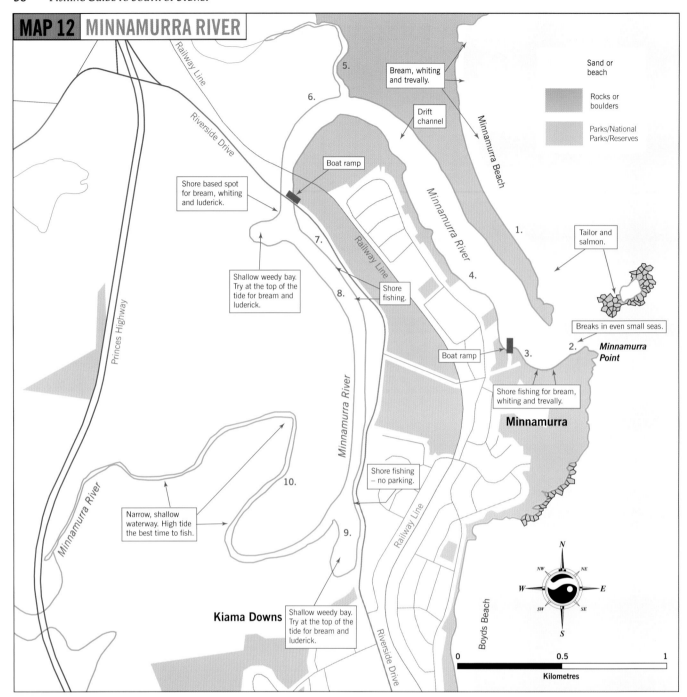

MAP 12 MINNAMURRA RIVER

Sand or beach

Rocks or boulders

Parks/National Parks/Reserves

5.

6.

Bream, whiting and trevally.

Drift channel

Boat ramp

Shore based spot for bream, whiting and luderick.

7.

Shallow weedy bay. Try at the top of the tide for bream and luderick.

8.

Shore fishing.

Boat ramp

Minnamurra River

Minnamurra Beach

1.

Tailor and salmon.

Breaks in even small seas.

2. *Minnamurra Point*

3.

Shore fishing for bream, whiting and trevally.

Minnamurra

Minnamurra River

10.

Narrow, shallow waterway. High tide the best time to fish.

Shore fishing – no parking.

9.

Minnamurra River

Railway Line

Princes Highway

Railway Line

Riverside Drive

Kiama Downs

Shallow weedy bay. Try at the top of the tide for bream and luderick.

Boyds Beach

Riverside Drive

N NW NE W E SW SE S

0   0.5   1
Kilometres

MAP 12 MINNAMURRA RIVER

The Minnamurra River enters the ocean adjacent to the northern side of Minnamurra Point, approximately 5 km north of Kiama Harbour. The main estuarine channels are typically less than 3 m deep. The river is tidal to the upper reaches of Terragong Swamp, which is 10 km from the entrance. Channel straightening within Terragong Swamp has been undertaken in the past and this has influenced the river hydraulics and sediment processes. The river meanders between Terragong Swamp and the sea.

The upper reaches of the Minnamurra River are great for bass fishing. Usually from September to May you can get the bass on Diving lures or surface lures. When there are plenty of bugs around just on dark using a surface lure should produce some fish. We strongly recommend catch and release for Australian bass. Another place bass can be found in our area is Jerrara Dam

located in Jamberoo. Several years ago NSW Fisheries along with the Department of primary industries stocked the dam with several thousand bass.

12.1   MINNAMURRA BEACH

See 11.2 page 36.

12.2   MINNAMURRA RIVER ENTRANCE

When the water is crystal clear here you can see a variety of fish species swimming around the entrance to the Minnamurra River and believe me they are very hard to catch. I have found the best time to fish here is very early morning, a couple of hours before the

This yellowfin bream took the TT Switchblade while the author was working the mangrove shoreline opposite the picnic tables in the Minnamurra River.

sun sets, at night and on an overcast day. This will usually make the fish less spooky. Try using live beach and blood worms, live nippers and poddy mullet. Whiting, dusky flathead, bream and silver trevally can be caught here.

12.3   BOAT RAMP

This area here is the same as spot 12.2 and it too can be fished quite successfully from the shore. Best fishing occurs during the run-up tide. You could also try using a few soft plastics for the dusky flathead that hold up here on the run-out tide.

12.4   SAND FLATS

Anchor either on top of the sand flats at high tide and fish half of the run-out tide or anchor at the edge of the sand banks and fish both the run-up and run out tides for whiting, bream and flathead.

12.5   SMALL CREEK

This small and shallow creek can only be fished near the top of the tide with small boats, canoes and kayaks for luderick, bream, whiting, dusky flathead, mullet and garfish. Try fishing with either no lead or very little. Float fishing works here as well. Live nipper, worms and poddy mullet are the go. Lure and soft plastics fishing are great fun here on both tides. Try the entrance to the creek on the run-out tide.

12.6   THE HOLE

Bream, flathead and luderick can be targeted here on all tides. Float fishing for the luderick, use a

sinker, swivel and a long leader for the bream and try the ball sinker directly onto the bait for the flathead. Soft plastics and metal vibes or blades work here as well.

12.7   PICNIC TABLES

You can park you car near the tables that are found here and walk down to the edge of the bank and fish for bream, whiting and dusky

ABOVE: The boat ramp beside the bridge at Minnamurra will give you easy access to the river and you can also fish from the shore here. Great place to take the kids.

BELOW: Lachlan Dubois just loves fishing out of his dad's Hobie Mirage Kyak. The Minnamurra River is an ideal spot for kayaks.

ABOVE: The father and son team of Rob and Andrew Humphries with a feed of fish that were caught while using soft plastics.

RIGHT: The Minnamurra River can be extremely clear at times and it doesn't seem to discourage the dusky flathead from grabbing a well presented hard bodied lure.

flathead. It is not a big cast that will get you to the sand and mud flats on the other side of the river, but you will need to watch out for boats. I have cast soft plastics from this side of the river to the flats at low tide and worked them over the edge of the drop-off for dusky flathead.

12.8   THE MANGROVES

Anchor here on a run-up tide for bream, dusky flathead, tailor and whiting. Small toads can be a nuisance here. Try berleying to get the fish to the boat.

12.9   WEEDY BAY

Virtually this whole bay has a weedy bottom. Great place to drift and cast soft plastics and small hard bodied lures for bream, whiting and dusky flathead.

12.10   SANDFLY ALLEY

As the names states, don't forget to take the insect spray. The sand flies will eat you alive at times, but the fishing can outweigh that problem. Fish for dusky flathead, whiting, bream and mullet. Bait, lures and soft plastics work here.

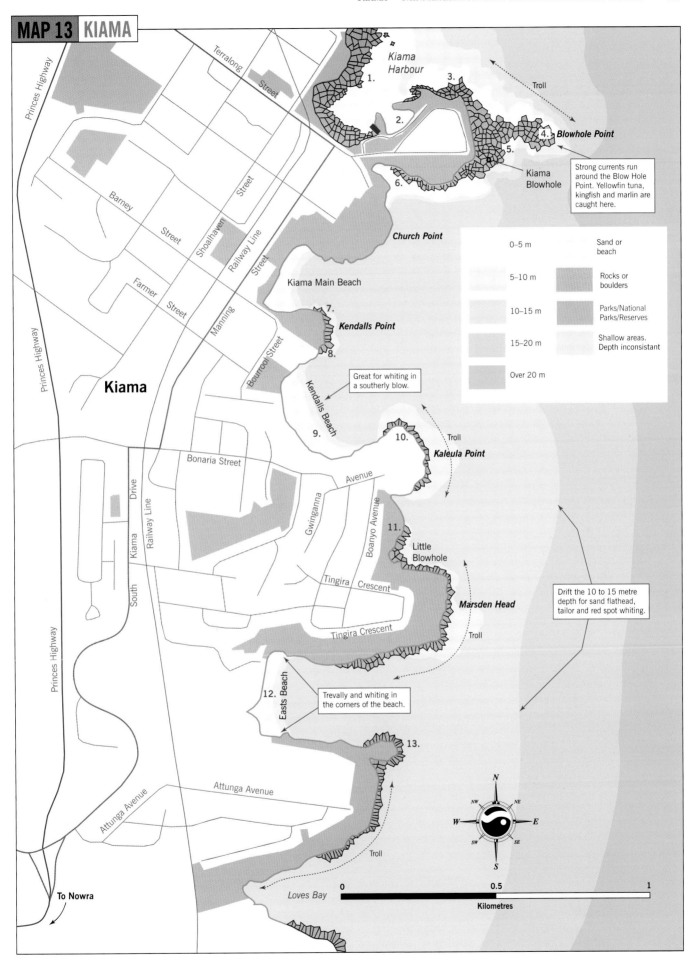

MAP 13 KIAMA

Princes Highway

Terralong   Street

Kiama Harbour

1.

3.

2.

4. ***Blowhole Point***

5.

Kiama Blowhole

6.

Strong currents run around the Blow Hole Point. Yellowfin tuna, kingfish and marlin are caught here.

Troll

Barney   Street

Shoalhaven   Street

Railway Line

Church Point

Kiama Main Beach

Farmer   Street

Manning   Street

Bourrool Street

Kiama

7.

Kendalls Point

8.

Kendalls Beach

9.

Great for whiting in a southerly blow.

	Sand or beach
0–5 m	
5–10 m	Rocks or boulders
10–15 m	Parks/National Parks/Reserves
15–20 m	Shallow areas. Depth inconsistant
Over 20 m	

Bonaria Street

Kiama   Drive

Railway Line

South

10.

Troll

Kaleula Point

Gwinganna

Avenue

Boanyo Avenue

11.

Little Blowhole

Tingira   Crescent

Marsden Head

Tingira Crescent

Troll

Drift the 10 to 15 metre depth for sand flathead, tailor and red spot whiting.

Easts Beach

12.

Trevally and whiting in the corners of the beach.

13.

Attunga Avenue

Attunga Avenue

Troll

N
NW   NE
W   E
SW   SE
S

Loves Bay

To Nowra

0	0.5	1

Kilometres

MAP 13 KIAMA

Long treasured as a holiday destination, Kiama has managed to maintain its charm as a casual, relaxing resort without falling the way of the high-rise compromise which has spoilt other areas. The sort of holiday place that the whole family can enjoy awaits visitors here.

Kiama's most famous feature is its 'blowhole' situated on Blowhole Point behind the point's lighthouse. Attracting thousands of visitors each year, this is a rock formation at the edge of the sea which sends plumes of water high into the air as the fierce waves surge through the hole in the rocks and release their energy with a spectacular show of the power of nature.

The local fishing fleet has its wharves on the northern side of Blowhole Point and there is no better place to taste the local seafood at its freshest.

The natural environment around this pretty town offers walks along pristine beaches, around fascinating rocky outcrops and through lush peaceful rainforest. Kiama has a colourful and varied commercial centre with all you'll need during your stay. A good variety of retail and eating outlets cater to all preferences and budgets. The most noted of Kiama's shops are the row of nineteenth century terrace houses which have been converted into craft outlets with something for everyone.

13.1   INSIDE PHEASANT POINT

You can park you car in Pheasant Street and walk to the fairly flat rock platform and fish for drummer, bream, silver trevally, luderick on a rising tide. Try using bread, peeled prawns, pilly tails and strips of mullet and tuna for bait. You can also cast metal lures and whole pilchards and garfish for tailor, Australian salmon and jewfish late in the afternoon or first thing in the morning.

13.2   BLACK BEACH

Try here for squid, garfish and mullet when there is not much wash around. When the seas are up and the waves are breaking on the

BELOW: Try fishing here for your live yellowtail, mullet and garfish.

taken when fishing as the swell does wrap around the point. High speed spinning or live baiting is the go from here. You can also try casting out whole pilchards and garfish for tailor, silver trevally and Australian salmon. Tourists and anglers have been washed in, so take care.

13.5 THE COVE

At times when the seas are up you can fish off the higher rocks for drummer, bream and silver trevally. You will need to berley with a mixture of bread, tuna oil and chicken pellets for the best results. I have found that fishing in the afternoon is best, especially when the shadows start to form on the water and there is a bit of white water about.

13.6 SURF BEACH

Surf Beach is Kiama's main surfing beach surrounded by parkland and central to Kiama's main shopping district. It is patrolled in summer and on weekends from the October long weekend through to Easter. Plenty of accessible car parking, toilets, barbecue facilities, picnic tables and changing sheds. Accessed off Manning St, Kiama.

13.7 KENDALLS

During the winter months this is a good spot after a blow to target snapper, drummer and bream. You can also fish during the summer months for bream and whiting in the sandy corner just north of the point. Pink nipper, beach and blood worms are the go.

13.8 SPLASHY

This platform fishes the same as Kendalls, especially if the wind is coming in from the northerly direction. It is only a short walk south.

13.9 KENDALLS BEACH

Kendalls Beach is an area of coastal land approximately a kilometer to the south of the town centre of the business centre of Kiama. It is set in a protected bay between Kendalls Point to the north and Kaleula Head to the south-east. A small but gorgeous beach, with amazing rock formations, it is a popular swimming spot for families and is known for its small surf. BBQ and playground facilities available.

ABOVE: Fish the deep water off the end of the rock platform on the northern side of the Blowhole at Kiama.

small beach you can try for silver trevally and bream on a rising tide. Berley is essential for the best results. You can also try fishing adjacent to the boat ramp that is in the corner near the take way shop.

13.3 THE POOL

Fish off the rocks on a rising tide for drummer, luderick and bream. To get the best results you will need to berley with bread, chopped up pilchards and chicken pellets. Fish with a float or a small ball sinker down onto the bait. Very snaggy off here. Try cunje, strips of tuna and mullet, whole or half pilchards, peeled blue tailed prawns and pink nippers for bait.

13.4 BLOWHOLE POINT

This little peninsula is a very popular spot for snapper, tuna, kingfish and the occasional jewfish. Very deep water off the end of this point and care will need to be

RIGHT: This rock finger is located on the northern side of the car park at the Blowhole.

13.10 MARSDENS HEAD

In winter the trevally are usually really thick here. Berley with pilchards, bread and chicken pellets. I have caught trevally to 1.5 kilos at times here. Mixed in with the trevally will be drummer, luderick, snapper and bream. You can also try spinning or live baiting here for tailor, Australian salmon, kingfish and tuna.

13.11 LITTLE BLOWHOLE

Great place to target bream, drummer and luderick on a rising tide. You can fish here with a bobby cork, float or a lightly weighted rig. Also try casting out a paternoster rig to the sandy bottom for bream, snapper and the odd jewfish on a rising tide.

The entrance to Kiama Harbour is a good place to target luderick and bream.

13.12 EASTS BEACH

A large, quiet, unpatrolled beach, generally protected from heavy seas by two headlands. Accessed by a short walk off Marsden St, Kiama this lovely beach for children with low, long sets of small waves and a small lagoon running into the beach.

13.13 HIGH CLIFFS

As the name applies it is high here and you will need to take a cliff gaff with you for when you are landing fish. Bream, drummer, snapper, silver trevally, tailor, Australian salmon and kingfish can be caught here throughout the year.

MAP 14 WERRI BEACH TO SEVEN MILE BEACH (SOUTH)

Gerringong and Gerroa are coastal villages with great views, great beaches and friendly locals. Close by you can spend a day visiting the wildlife refuge, home to kangaroos, emus, wombats and many more of Australia's fantastic native flora and fauna, including our colourful parrots.

South of Gerroa stretches the magnificent Seven Mile Beach. This spectacular beach is protected within its own National Park and is backed by beautiful stands of our grand forests and other native vegetation. Wonderful views of the expanse of this beach and its park can be appreciated from the northern entrance to Gerroa.

There is a range of accommodation in the two towns. Restaurants and clubs provide fine food and entertainment for visitors.

Jamberoo, a little west of the other towns, is something different again. A rural village surrounded by lush dairy farms, it charms with its historic buildings and country atmosphere. Just a few kilometres north of the town is a year round recreation park. Grass skiing with chairlift is one of the most popular attractions along with waterslides, bobsleds, racing cars, minigolf and more. Just west of Jamberoo is the beautiful Minnamurra Rainforest Park, part of the Budderoo National Park and hosting a rainforest education centre and boardwalks into this precious environment.

Beyond Minnamurra Falls is a nature reserve popular with bird watchers and with head lands in stark contrast to the coastal strip.

At the northern end of Seven Mile Beach you will find the entrance to the Crooked River and a beach boat ramp.

14.1 WERRI LAGOON

This is a very small and shallow lagoon that will produce poddy mullet, garfish and at times bream and dusky flathead. Most of the time the lagoon is closed to the open sea, but when it is open the beach is a great place to target whiting, bream, flathead, tailor and Australian salmon on the run-out tide. Pink nipper, squirt worms, pilly tails and strips of mullet are the go for bait. You could also try using beach, blood and tube worms. Jewfish can also be caught here at night or just after a big sea has started to abate.

14.2 THE BLUFF

Park in the small car park at the northern end of Werri Beach, walk across the sand to the headland. This may sometimes be cut off by the creek opening and you may have to wade through the water at shin height. You will then need to walk around the back of the headland and you will come across a small shell beached cove. It is on either side of this cove that you can fish for bream, drummer, luderick, silver trevally, tailor, groper and the odd snapper and kingfish. At low tide you can gather for bait, crabs, cunje, green weed and cabbage.

14.3 WERRI BEACH

Werri is a forever-changing beach providing good gutters and channels. Parking is available all along Pacific Avenue. Salmon and tailor are prolific during the winter months, especially at dawn and dusk. Pilchards on gang hooks are probably the best bait to use. Summer produces bream, whiting and flathead. Bream are more prevalent towards both the north and south ends of the beach near

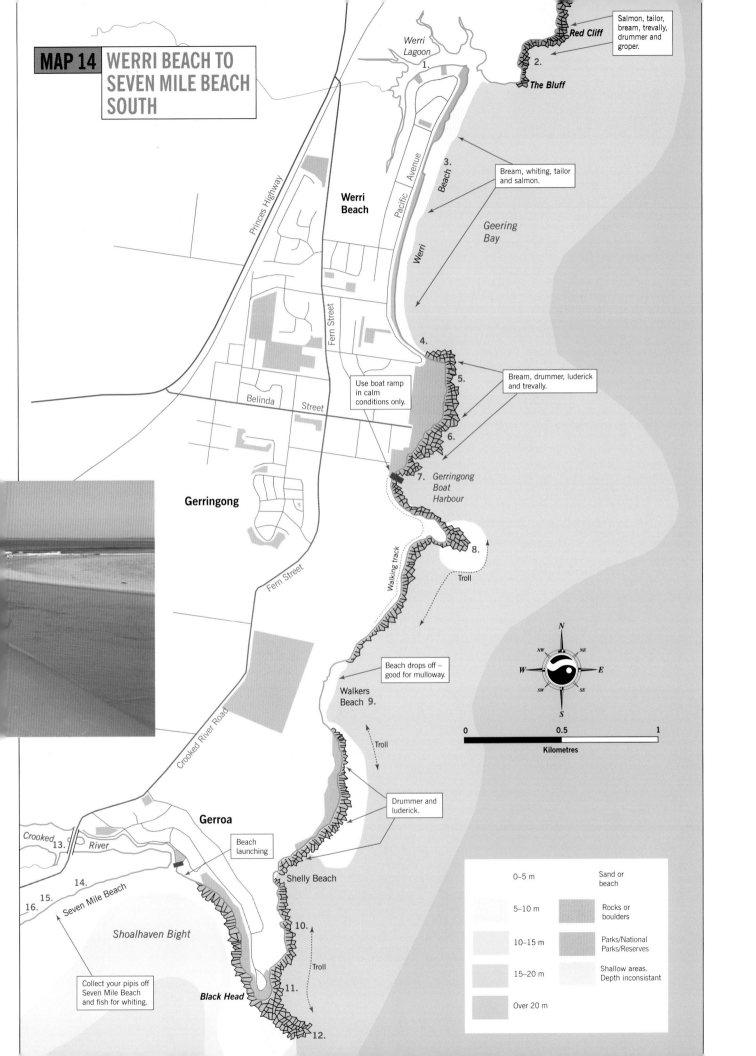

MAP 14 WERRI BEACH TO SEVEN MILE BEACH SOUTH

Werri Lagoon

1.

Red Cliff

Salmon, tailor, bream, trevally, drummer and groper.

2.

The Bluff

3.

Bream, whiting, tailor and salmon.

Werri Beach

Werri Beach

Pacific Avenue

Werri Beach

Geering Bay

Princes Highway

Fern Street

4.

5.

Bream, drummer, luderick and trevally.

Gerringong

Belinda Street

Use boat ramp in calm conditions only.

6.

7. *Gerringong Boat Harbour*

Walking track

8.

Troll

Fern Street

Beach drops off – good for mulloway.

Walkers Beach 9.

Troll

Gerroa

Drummer and luderick.

Crooked River Road

Beach launching

Crooked River

13.

14.

15.

16.

Seven Mile Beach

Shelly Beach

10.

Shoalhaven Bight

Troll

11.

Collect your pipis off Seven Mile Beach and fish for whiting.

Black Head

12.

Compass: N, NW, NE, W, E, SW, SE, S

0   0.5   1
Kilometres

0–5 m	Sand or beach
5–10 m	Rocks or boulders
10–15 m	Parks/National Parks/Reserves
15–20 m	Shallow areas. Depth inconsistant
Over 20 m	

the rocky points. Mulloway can be found most of the year at night. You can also try beach worming towards the middle of the beach where it is usually a bit flatter.

14.4 THE ALLEY

This corner of the beach is very similar to the alley that is at Cronulla in Sydney. It is a place where surf board riders will use currents that will carry them out to the back of the great waves that break here. As an angler you can use these same currents to get your berley and bait out to the deeper holes where the bream, tailor, Australian salmon, and whiting lie in wait. During the winter months I have also caught luderick and drummer here on cunje and peeled prawns.

14.5 THE POOL

This headland can provide two types of rock fishing in the one area. Parking is available at the point. The northern rock platform adjacent to the swimming pools provides a good area for luderick, drummer and bream. Bait can be green weed, cunje, cabbage or prawns. Luderick and drummer appear to be more prevalent on the rising tide. The eastern side provides a typical rock fishing area, with salmon, tailor, luderick, drummer and bream all in the one spot. Care should be taken when fishing here.

14.6 SPLASHY

As the name suggest it can get a bit wet at this section of rock platform. Best fished when the seas are slight to very calm. Plenty of squid, drummer, luderick, bream and silver trevally can be berleyed up here on a rising tide. You can also cast out those metal lures for tailor, Australian salmon and the odd bonito.

14.7 BOAT HARBOUR

Located at the eastern end of Jupiter Street, this ramp is open to the sea and is affected by both high tides and the swell, especially from the north-east. Potential users are encouraged to check with experienced locals before using it. We suggest you make yourself familiar with alternative boat ramps in the area, in case a high swell prevents re-entry. Ensure you have sufficient fuel to reach an alternative. The ramp has ample parking, fish cleaning facilities, picnic area and amenities.

When the seas are up so high that you can't fish from any one of the rock or beach formations in the area, this is the place to come to. I have caught drummer, silver trevally, bream, tailor, groper and mullet here. You must berley and fish from the top of the tide to about halfway down for the best results.

14.8 BOAT HARBOUR HEADLAND

This small, but at times very productive headland has it all. You can fish the washes for drummer, bream, silver trevally and luderick or chase Australian salmon, tailor and bonito with whole ganged pilchards and metal lures. Snapper and morwong can also be targeted here with the humble paternoster rig. Care will need to be taken when the seas are up, but there is fairly deep water around most of the headland. To get to the headland you can either walk the tracks south and over the top or just walk around the front, but be aware that the high tide will cut the rock platform off to the headland.

14.9 WALKERS BEACH

A beautiful beach that requires a walk down and across the golf course to get to. It is the return uphill journey that usually is unwelcome, especially if you end up with a good catch. Entry via this access is legal. A small off-road parking area is at the northern end of the golf course, on Fern Street. Please keep to the fairways (normal grass) and fence-line as much as possible. Salmon and tailor are good at the beach, with mulloway at night.

14.10 THE BLUE HOLE

If you park your car in Headland Drive at Gerroa and walk the pathway through the houses to the rocks you will be able to follow a path over the to point called the Blue Hole. Most of the water depth around this platform is fairly deep, but there are a number of shallow and flat areas that can be covered with water at high tide. So care will need to be taken when fishing here.

Drummer, bream, silver trevally, bonito, Australian salmon, tailor, kingfish and tuna can be caught here. There is not a lot of natural bait to be found so you will need to bring in most of your bait. It can get very dangerous when there is a sea running. Try fishing when the shadows are on the water for the best results. You can also walk from here north to Walkers Beach.

14.11 THE CUT AWAY

There is a small cut away in the rock platform that can at times be very productive for bream and

Crooked River at Gerroa may not hold a lot of water, but it is still worth a shot for dusky flathead, luderick and mullet when the tide is high.

The Blue Hole is located just north of Black Head at Gerroa.

drummer, but you will need to have plenty of white water. Fish here with either a small float or a small ball sinker that goes right down onto the bait.

14.12 BLACK HEAD

This rock platform is where I first learnt to fish from rocks. To me it has just about everything a rock angler is after. High speed spinning for pelagics, live baiting for kingfish and tuna. Snapper and groper fishing out a bit wider. Wash fishing for bream, silver trevally and drummer. Float fishing for luderick.

Even though this rock platform may look very safe in calm conditions you will still need to take care when fishing here as it is exposed to the ocean currents and there is a small bombora just to the south. At high tide the stretch of boulders that are between the headland and the rock platform will be covered with water. The depth does vary, so don't get trapped on the headland and have to wait until the tide recedes.

14.13 CROOKED RIVER

On the northern side of Crooked River there is a small concrete ramp that is usually covered by firm sand and therefore not visible, virtually making the ramp facility a "beach launch". The ramp is really only suitable for smaller craft, but it can give to access to great offshore fishing areas. If you have never launched out through the surf you will need to go and talk to the anglers at Gerroa Boat Fisherman's club and they will tell you the "dos and don'ts" of launching from here. Unformed parking is available on the sand under the cliff face.

This river is subject to natural silting and closing from time to time. The upper reaches provide good bream and flathead. It is also a good prawning area. The mud flats provide live bait. Fishing is usually from the bank, canoe or light "tinny" as the river does not have ramp access.

14.14 THE CARAVAN PARK

The caravan park leads to a natural scenic coastal beach that stretches for seven miles from Gerroa in the north through to Shoalhaven Heads in the south. The beach is renowned for its safe surf and is used for a number of surfing schools throughout the summer season. Access to the northern end is via Riverleigh Avenue and Burke Parade with parking, toilets and picnic facilities over the footbridge. Entry points and parking are also available further south after crossing the Crooked River Bridge. The northern end is patrolled in summer on weekends from the long weekend in October through to Easter.

This is a good beach for salmon and tailor during the winter months and bream and whiting during summer. This is an easy beach to locate batches of pipis for use as fresh bait. It should be remembered that it is illegal to take pipis off the beach but legal to use them on the beach as bait. Parking is provided in Burke Parade for access to Little and Seven Mile beaches. There is also parking and access to the beach via tracks through the hinterland all along Crooked River Road, south of the bridge.

14.15 THE TIP

Access to this section of Seven Mile Beach can be gained by walking south from the caravan park entrance or the track just south of the local tip. Once here you can gather pipis and beach worms and fish for whiting, bream, flathead, flounder, Australian salmon and tailor. Other great baits to try are sea garfish, pilchards, tuna and mullet strips. You can also target jewfish in one of the many deep holes that can be found here, but remember they may be there one day and gone the next.

14.16 BEACH ROAD

If you drive to the end of Beach Road you will come to a picnic area that has plenty of parking and toilets. It is from here you can either walk north or south to locate the gutters and holes. Fish for Australian salmon, tailor, bream, whiting, flathead and jewfish on a rising tide.

MAP 15 WOLLONGONG TO SHOALHAVEN HEADS
— OFFSHORE GPS SPOTS

Kiama has some great game fishing both offshore and land based, more particularly from September through to May. For game fishing off the boats, we often see captures from the Kiama Canyons and from around the Mount Fuji fish traps species such as: black marlin, striped marlin, yellowfin tuna, albacore, kingfish, dolphin fish and a range of sharks. Most commonly used tackle for game fishing in the area is 15-24kg tackle. Trolling lures such as skirted lures, Xmas Tree lures, bibbless minnow lures, Rapala lures and Squidgies Bluewater Live Series soft plastic lures all work well. Land based game fishing is also quite popular off Kiama Blowhole point and Marsdens Headland with the use of live baits floated out under a balloon.

Off Kiama Reefs you can catch many fish species. Some of the more popular targets are snapper and morwong. Along the sand flats just out of the Kiama Harbour and across to Minnamurra — Bass Point it can often pay to stay in close and drift as when the flathead are around, there is sure to be a good number!

If you are visiting the area Kiama has a few charter boats that operate out of Kiama Harbour. The skippers know the good fishing spots and will put you onto some good catches should you book a trip with them.

15.1   BANDIT REEF
S 34 18 733   E 151 02 491

7 nautical miles from Bellambi. 8.5 nautical miles from Wollongong. 17 fathoms deep.

Marlin, tuna, kingfish, snapper, morwong, cobia, samson fish, pig fish and leatherjackets.

15.2   BULLI SANDS
S 34 19 735   E 150 59 012

17 to fathoms. Eastern mark drops off to about 24 fathoms. 4 nautical miles Bellambi. Best flathead grounds of the northern suburb. Inner Sands 20 fathoms. Outer Sands 25 fathoms.

15.3   WOLLONGONG EAST SHELF
S 34 28 800   E 151 15 000

16 nautical miles east in 110 fathoms. Yellowfin and marlin

15.4   SPINKS REEF
S 34 23 200   E 150 55 650

1.5 nautical miles from Bellambi boat ramp in 10 fathoms. Snapper, silver trevally, jewfish, samson fish, cobia, bream and baitfish.

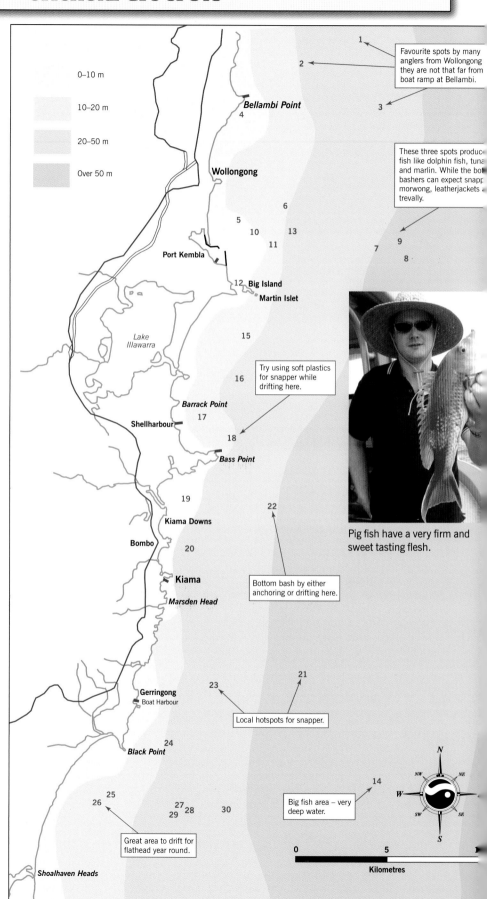

0–10 m

10–20 m

20–50 m

Over 50 m

Bellambi Point
4

Wollongong

6
5
10   13
11

Port Kembla

12 Big Island
Martin Islet

15

16

Lake Illawarra

Barrack Point
17

Shellharbour

18

Bass Point

19

Kiama Downs

Bombo

20

Kiama

Marsden Head

22

Gerringong
Boat Harbour

23

21

24

Black Point

14

25
26

27 28
29   30

Shoalhaven Heads

1
2

3

Favourite spots by many anglers from Wollongong they are not that far from boat ramp at Bellambi.

These three spots produce fish like dolphin fish, tuna and marlin. While the bottom bashers can expect snapper, morwong, leatherjackets and trevally.

7   9
8

Try using soft plastics for snapper while drifting here.

Pig fish have a very firm and sweet tasting flesh.

Bottom bash by either anchoring or drifting here.

Local hotspots for snapper.

Big fish area – very deep water.

Great area to drift for flathead year round.

N
NW   NE
W   E
SW   SE
S

0   5
Kilometres

ABOVE: Australian salmon can be trolled up during the summer months while working the washes close to Big Island.

LEFT: Blue morwong are commonly caught throughout the reefs that are situated off the coast from Wollongong to Shoalhaven Heads.

15.5 BOMBO WRECK
S 24 26 800   E 150 55 600

2.5 nautical miles from Port Kembla. 13 fathoms. General reef fish species, jewfish, snapper, silver trevally, john dory, morwong, pig fish and leatherjackets.

15.6 WOLLONGONG REEF
S 34 26 470   E 150 57 590

4.5 nautical miles north-east of Port Kembla. 6 nautical miles north of Shellharbour. 16 fathom peak. Snapper, tuna, marlin, kingfish, jewfish and morwong.

15.7 WAVERIDER BUOY
S 34 28 660   E 151 01 510

6 nautical miles out from Port Kembla. 50 fathoms deep. Dolphin fish, tuna, kingfish and snapper.

15.8 RANGERS REEF
S 34 29 240   E 151 04 230

9.5 nautical miles from Port Kembla. 69 fathoms. Snapper, marlin, kingfish, sweep, morwong and tuna.

15.9 PORT TRAPS
S 34 28 350   E 151 03 390

8.5 nautical miles from Port Kembla. 56 fathoms. Snapper, morwong, pig fish, kingfish, silver trevally, leatherjackets and dolphin fish.

15.10 FLINDERS ISLAND (TOOTH BRUSH ISLAND) S 34 27 500   E 150 55 800

2 nautical miles from Port Kembla. 4 to 9 fathoms. Anchor and berley heavily for bream, silver trevally and drummer on a rising tide. Take care of which way the swell is coming from.

15.11 BASS ISLAND (PIG ISLAND)
S 34 27 900   E 150 56 800

3 nautical miles from Port Kembla. 5 to 15 fathoms. Fish the front eastern point for kingfish, bream, silver trevally and leatherjackets. Fish in close to the washes for bream, drummer, luderick and tailor. You could also try trolling around the island for tailor, Australian salmon and kingfish.

15.12 BIG ISLAND
S 34 29 500   E 150 55 900

3.5 nautical miles from Port Kembla. 6 to 12 fathoms. Troll around the south-eastern corner of the island for tuna, kingfish, Australian salmon and tailor. The north-western corner of the island produces tailor, Australian salmon and snapper. Try floating out a whole pilchard or using live yellowtail and slimy mackerel

15.13 PORT KEMBLA 12 MILE
S 34 29 240   E 151 04 220

12 nautical miles from Shellharbour. 64 fathoms. Dolphin fish, tuna, kingfish, snapper and morwong.

15.14 KIAMA CANYON N/E
S 34 47 590   E 151 10 590

17 nautical miles from Kiama, 23 nautical miles from Greenwell Point. 150 fathoms.
Winter—gemfish, blueye trevalla. Summer—shark, marlin, yellowfin tuna.
Water depth 260–380m. Broken bottom reef & pinnacles to the edge of shelf.

15.15 ONE TREE
S 34 31 200   E 150 54 300

2 nautical miles from Shellharbour. 13 fathoms, snapper, morwong, silver trevally and other reef species.

15.16 WINDANG WIDE
S 34 33 090   E 150 55 300

3 nautical miles north-east of Shellharbour. 28 fathoms. General reef fishing.

Try targeting dolphin fish with Tropic Angler skirted lures at The Paddock.

A nice pair of chinaman leatherjackets.

15.17 CHURCH GROUNDS
S 34 34 800   E 150 54 000

1 nautical mile east of Shellharbour. 13 to 14 fathoms. Jewfish, bream, silver trevally, cobia, snapper, morwong, sweep, kingfish and leatherjackets.

15.18 THE HUMPS
S 34 35 600   E 150 54 600

1.5 nautical miles from Shellharbour, just north of Bass Point. 18 fathoms. Fish here for general reef fish species. Try either drifting with a paternoster rig or anchor and berley, while using either paternoster rigs or ball sinkers directly on top of the bait.

15.19 MINNAMURRA REEF
S 34 37 250   E 150 52 700

3.5 nautical miles from Shellharbour and Kiama boat ramp. 10 fathoms. Kingfish, snapper, bream, silver trevally, jewfish and pig fish.

15.20 FLATHEAD DRIFT
S 34 39 400   E 15 52 800

2 nautical miles from Kiama is this is a great place to drift for flathead in 17 to 19 fathoms of water.

15.21 MOUNT FUJI
S 34 43 090   E 150 59 320

10 nautical miles from Shellharbour. 55 fathoms for general reef fishing.

15.22 THE PADDOCK
S 34 37 800   E 150 56 400

3 nautical miles south-east of Bass Point 38 to 45 fathoms. Bottom bash for morwong, snapper, kingfish and leatherjackets. Troll this same area for tuna, marlin and kingfish.

15.23 GERRINGONG GRASSLANDS
S 34 44 220   E 150 56 210

10 nautical miles south from Bass Point. 58 fathoms. Pig fish, snapper, morwong, kingfish and leatherjackets

15.24 GERROA
S 34 46 700   E 150 52 700

10 nautical miles from Greenwell Point, 2 nautical miles from Boat Harbour at Gerringong. 30 fathoms. Broken reef, gravel and sand patches. Flathead, snapper, morwong, leatherjackets and the odd kingfish.

15.25 THE TIP SITE
S 34 49 420   E 150 48 670

This area is located about 2 to 3 nautical miles off the surf shed at Shoalhaven Heads and is a great place to drift for flathead. Snapper, tailor, Australian salmon, leatherjackets and kingfish can also be caught here at times

15.26 FLATHEAD DRIFT
S 34 49 428   E 150 49 639

Drift about 3 to 4 nautical miles off the beach at Gerroa for flathead, flounder, snapper and tailor.

Try cubing for yellowfin tuna off Wollongong Reef.

This chinaman leatherjacket was just over 2.3 kilos.

15.27 MISSION GROUNDS
S 34 50 573   E 150 54 346

This small broken reef and sand is about 6 nautical miles from Boat Harbour at Gerringong. Marlin, tuna, kingfish, dolphin fish and snapper can be caught here.

15.28 BERRY TURN-OFF
S 34 50 650 E 150 54 390

6 nautical miles from Boat Harbour at Gerringong and about 9 nautical miles from Greenwell Point. 40 fathoms. Snapper, kingfish, morwong, sweep, pig fish and leatherjackets.

15.29 BANKS NORTH WALL
S 34 59 945   E 150 54 390

8 nautical miles from Shoalhaven heads and 13 nautical miles from Boat Harbour at Gerringong. Marlin, yellowfin tuna, kingfish and snapper. Try drifting edges of banks for flathead and leatherjackets.

15.30 100 FATHOM MARK
S 34 55 860   E 151 05 170

17 nautical miles south of Boat Harbour. Marlin, yellowfin tuna, kingfish and snapper. Try drifting the edges of the banks for flathead and leatherjackets.

BOAT RAMPS KIAMA—MINNAMURRA RIVER TO SEVEN MILE BEACH AT GERROA

Name	Make	Condition	No of Lanes	Wash Down	Lights	Fish Clean	BBQ	Toilets
Map 12 Minnamurra River								
Charles Ave Minnamurra	Concrete	Good	1	No	Yes	No	Yes	Yes
Minnamurra River Entrance	Concrete	Good	1	No	No	No	Yes	Yes
John Holts Reserve Minnamurra	Concrete	Good	1	Yes	No	No	Yes	Yes
Map 13 Kiama								
Terralong Street Kiama	Concrete	Excellent	2	Yes	Yes	Yes	Yes	yes
Map 14 Werri Beach to Seven Mile Beach (south)								
Bourke Street Gerroa	Beach Sand	Poor	nil	No	No	No	No	No
Jupiter Street Gerringong	Concrete	Good	1	yes	yes	yes	yes	yes

TACKLE SHOPS KIAMA—MINNAMURRA RIVER TO SEVEN MILE BEACH AT GERROA

OCEAN STORM FISHING TACKLE
Shop 15, 106 Terralong Street Kiama
PHONE: (02) 4232 1876

Gerringong Bait, Tackle & Sports Store
142 Fern St Gerringong
PHONE: (02) 4234 1824

CHAPTER 3
SHOALHAVEN
Shoalhaven River and South to Warrain Beach at Currarong

ABOVE: The bridge that crosses the Shoalhaven River at Nowra

BELOW: Launching from a boat ramp near the bridge that crosses the Shoalhaven River at Nowra.

Shoalhaven City is a large area of mixed urban, rural and forested land anchored in the north by the significant twin towns of Nowra and Bomaderry, which sit on opposite banks of the mighty Shoalhaven River. Nowra is the largest coastal town on the NSW south coast beyond Wollongong, and is the business and administrative centre of the fast-growing Shoalhaven region.

The Shoalhaven River is one of the most significant systems south of Sydney, rising far to the south west near Araluen and Braidwood. It flows north then east through rugged gorge country and joins the Kangaroo River to form the backed-up waters of Lake Yarrunga (Tallowa Dam), before twisting eastward across the rich alluvial flood plains around Nowra and Bomaderry. It ultimately empties into the sea at Greenwell Point, after joining the much smaller Crookhaven River via the convict-dug Berrys Canal that links these two systems. This effectively ensures that the Shoalhaven's historic mouth at Shoalhaven Head remains shut for at least 95 per cent of the time.

The Shoalhaven district boasts a wide range of popular natural attractions. As well as its many magnificent beaches and waterways, the northern part of the Shoalhaven region takes in Jervis Bay, Kangaroo Valley, Ettrema Wilderness, the Budawang Ranges, expansive Morton National Park, St Georges Basin and Sussex Inlet, to name just a handful of the better-known locations.

The southern end of the Shoalhaven features the very popular holiday destinations of Milton and Ulladulla and their beautiful surrounding districts, known loosely as "The Coastal Resort". The year-round holiday resorts of Mollymook, Narrawallee, Burrill Lake and Lake Tabourie are all nestled in this area. In the far southern end of the region, the magnificent coastal-fringed Murramarang National Park is famous for its rugged shoreline and varied native wildlife. We will go into greater detail on these places and more in the coming chapters of this guide.

I lived on the Headland at Gerroa for 14 years and fished in the Shoalhaven at least once a week and I still have records of fish that I caught in the river that many years ago.

The Shoalhaven has plenty of spots for both the land based angler and those of you that own a boat. Try concentrating your fishing times to the quieter parts of the day or when it is a bit on the overcast side or raining.

Even though there are more restricted areas that you can't fish in Jervis Bay, there are still enough about to keep even the experienced angler onto fish. Marlin, kingfish, snapper, flathead, tailor, Australian salmon, whiting, tuna, luderick, drummer and bream are just some of the fish species that are still being caught in Jervis Bay.

If you are into chasing pelagics and reef fish species there are a number of ramps in Jervis Bay that will give you easy access to some great off shore fishing.

Accommodation and services to cater for all tastes and budgets are readily available throughout the Shoalhaven City district. This whole area has much to offer the resident and visiting recreational angler, as well as non-fishing family members or companions.

MAP 16 SHOALHAVEN RIVER ENTRANCE TO NOWRA BRIDGE

Shoalhaven Heads is located at the southern end of famous Seven Mile Beach and its surrounding National Park. It has some of the best surf on the south coast all through the year for both body and board surfers. The local surf life saving club provides beach patrols in the main holiday season. It has a modern surf club on the beach.

The neighbouring townships of Shoalhaven Heads and Coolangatta are popular destinations for visitors to the NSW south coast. Things to do and see are endless with the area being situated between ocean and river beaches, Coolangatta Mountain and Seven Mile Beach National Park. Nowra, Bomaderry and Berry are just minutes away with Kangaroo Valley and Jervis Bay within easy reach.

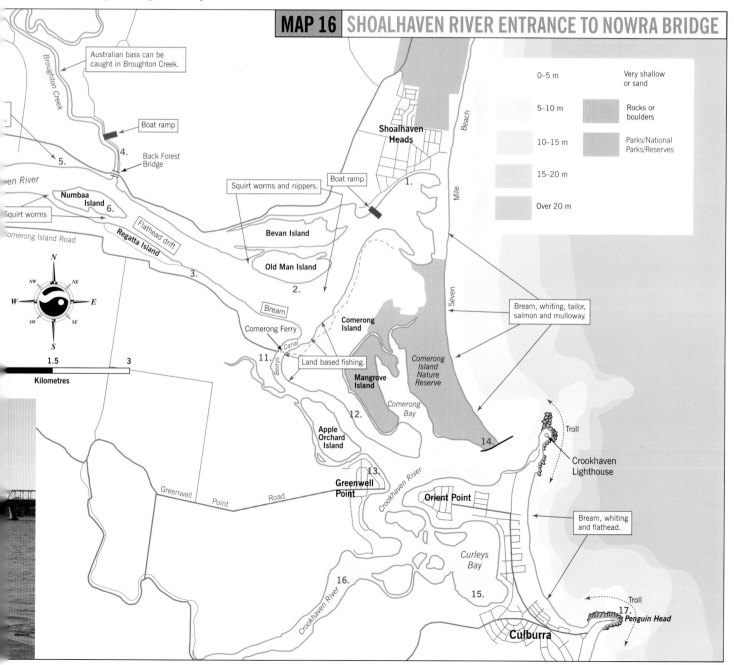

The Shoalhaven is the largest and most significant river of southern NSW. It rises between Braidwood and Araluen, flowing north and then east for over 400 kilometres, entering the sea near Greenwell Point.

The Shoalhaven near Nowra is broad, relatively shallow and dotted with sandbars, mud flats and reefs. Since the construction of a convict built canal linking the lower Shoalhaven with the Crookhaven River in the late nineteenth century, the natural river mouth at Shoalhaven Heads is often silted up and shut for many years at a time. I remember as a kid I was able to fish for bream, flathead, whiting, Australian salmon and tailor on a run-out tide here, but I haven't been able to do the same for over twenty years.

Crookhaven Heads is a coastal village a few kilometres from Culburra Beach. It is here that the Shoalhaven and Crookhaven Rivers run into the Tasman Sea. Superb access to one of Australia's finest deepwater and estuarine fishing areas. It has one of the regions biggest boat ramps.

16.1 SHOALHAVEN HEADS

For those of you that have boats there are vast areas of shallow flats and weed beds in this area that are worth prospecting for flathead, bream and whiting. Those of you that are restricted to fishing from the shore will need to put in a good cast to get out past the weed banks to the sandy areas where the fish are. Try drifting the stretch of shoreline leading into the village of Shoalhaven Heads, and the channel running right past the caravan park on the northern shore.

Flounder can't resist slowly worked soft plastics along the bottom or over the edge of a drop off.

16.2 OLD MAN ISLAND

This is a big sandy island flanked by deep weed beds leading to the junction of the river and the canal that has a vast nipper colony. Drift over this area at high tide for bream, whiting and mullet, but remember to fish as light as possible. Lures and soft plastics work well here.

The river splits here, with the bulk of the water heading south down into the Crookhaven system via the canal, and what's left of the Shoalhaven heading north and east towards Shoalhaven Heads. While drifting for dusky flathead in the deeper water I have caught small jewfish on strips of mullet.

16.3 THE SILO

Downstream from Regatta Creek, the big blue silo marks good drifting country for all species, but is one of my favourite spots to chase dusky flathead. The entrance to this tiny creek on the southern bank offers some great fishing for the first of the run out tide. Anchor at high tide near the entrance and take care not to get caught as the water is shallow and the mud is deep.

16.4 BROUGHTON CREEK

This creek enters the river on the northern side and is a pretty fair fishery. There is a gravel ramp about a kilometre up from the entrance, though parking is pretty limited. Broughton Creek holds some good fishing at times for bream, flathead and luderick, but plenty of nets get in there to spoil things. The mouth of the creek holds some good accessible bank fishing to the west, and limited access to the east. Though the current runs pretty hard on this bank there can be good bream, luderick and flathead around this area.

16.5 TUMBLE DOWN

This stretch of shoreline has a step set of banks that drops off into fairly deep water. When there has been a bit of a flood the shoreline can tumble down into the river. Bream, flathead, whiting and jewfish are caught off the shore from here.

16.6 NUMBAA ISLAND

This sandy island lies close to the southern bank opposite Broughton Creek and can provide good flats fishing for whiting, dusky flathead, bream and mullet. It is another place that you can pump for squirt worms and nippers. The river stretches from here down to the canal and offers good drifts for bream, flathead, whiting and flounder. You can also try anchoring close to the shoreline and lay out a small, but steady berley trail. I have caught plenty of luderick

This dusky flathead couldn't resist a tropic angler deep diver that was trolled along the shoreline at Numbaa Island.

here on a run-out tide while using squirt worms for bait. Jewfish will also frequent this stretch of water.

Just downstream from Pig Island lays an old graveyard, barely visible from the river. Locals will tell you however that the area near the graveyard is a good drift for flathead and whiting. From here down to the entrance to Broughton Creek there are broad areas of shallow flats and weed beds worth prospecting for flathead, bream and whiting.

16.7   GRANTS ROCKS

This small patch of hard reef lies on the northern bank opposite the channel at the end of Pig Island. The tidal eddies and currents can attract bream, large dusky flathead, mullet and luderick. I have found that you need to berley here with a combination of chopped up pilchards, bread and chicken pellets.

16.8   PAPER MILL

This mill lies on the northern bank opposite the bottom end of Pig Island. A hot water outlet pipe can attract

When targeting bream in the Shoalhaven River try anchoring and berleying at the Reef or Pig Island.

bream and luderick. The broad stretch of river in this area is worth a drift for flathead and whiting. There is an industrial complex on the northern bank that was once a real hotspot, with a berley of gluten concentrating the fish. Nowadays a white waste is pumped into the river, but does not seem to hold the same attraction for fish. Never-the-less bream mullet and blackfish do appear around here.

16.9   THE REEF AND PIG ISLAND

The Reef lies about 500m downstream from the bridge, and is close to the northern bank. The main channel is narrow and deep between the reef and the bank, and the tide fairly rips through there. Bream, luderick and the occasional school jew can be found around the reef. Just downstream from the reef is the mouth of Bomaderry Creek, where bream, luderick and flathead can be taken while fishing close to the shore.

Pig Island is the first big sand island down from the bridge, lying close to the southern bank. Flathead and whiting can be chased on the flats, and there are good supplies of squirt worms generally available. There is a narrow channel on the southern side of the island behind the village of Terara that fishes for bream, luderick, flathead and whiting, though the drain flowing in here from the local sewage processing plant can be a bit on the nose.

16.10   THE BRIDGES

Fishing around the pylons can turn up bream and flathead. The water is generally shallow on the southern side, with the deep channel close to the northern side. Try deep water jigging on the northern and southern sides of the bridge for bream, dusky flathead and the odd estuary perch. Just upstream from the bridge on the southern side there is a stretch of rocky shore situated below the cliffs on the southern bank, behind the hospital. There is very deep water here, and due to ski boat traffic, it is best fished at dawn or dusk. Bream, luderick and school jewfish tend to hang out here. There is an accessible bank on the southern side of the river, between the bridge and the cliffs.

16.11   O'KEEFE'S POINT

On the mainland side of the ferry this sandy point offers shore access for bream, flathead, whiting, and jew fishing. Further into the Canal to the south of the ferry there is good (though very snaggy) country for bream and luderick. If you catch the ferry over to Comerong Island you could fish plenty of good shoreline for the bank angler, with good luderick, bream and flathead country to the north of the ferry. You could also travel over to the beach at the back of the island and fish for bream, whiting, tailor, Australian salmon and jewfish.

16.12   THE CANAL

This stretch of river running though to Greenwell Point is lined in parts with oyster clad rock walls which offer good bream, whiting, dusky flathead and luderick fishing. The area of sunken rock walls on the southern bank is a prime spot. There are a number of floating oyster racks through here that are worth anchoring up near and berleying for bream, whiting and dusky flathead. You could also try fishing some of the creek entrances that come off Comerong Island on a run-out tide. Anchor or cast near where the water comes through the mangrove. Most of the canal stretch is boat country, although at Greenwell Point there is plenty of access for shore based anglers.

16.13   GREENWELL POINT

There are a couple of ramps here which give access to this lower end of the river system and there is shore access around the pool and the small park south of there. Fishing is also possible off the Greenwell Point jetty. The area can turn on bream, luderick, trevally, flathead and whiting, and the jetty is a good place to top up the livebait tanks.

Just up stream of the wharf, on the southern side there is a land based spot that is worth a shot for bream, whiting and dusky flathead with either live poddy mullet, pink nippers or blood worms. You can also target leatherjackets and luderick here as well.

16.14   CROOKHAVEN ENTRANCE

On the northern shore bordering Comerong Island there are some good flats and weed beds, and there is a long rock wall known as the Coal Wharf that is great for land based anglers, accessible via the canal ferry. The inner part of the wall is luderick country, and the outer wall can get you into tailor country, with bream, flathead, trevally and school jew possible.

On the southern shore there is the regional boat ramp at Crookhaven Heads that provides access to the water, and the rocky shoreline out to the entrance is worthwhile for luderick, bream and trevally.

16.15   CULBURRA

There are some shallow, mangrove-lined bays bordering Culburra to the east of Greenwell Point. Bream, luderick and flathead are all possible in this area. The shallows around Goodnight Island are worth working, as well as the areas close to oyster racks and pontoons.

16.16   CROOKHAVEN RIVER

The Crookhaven winds through mangrove country to the south of Greenwell Point and can hold some solid flathead. Try drifting and spinning along the stands of mangroves. This area is also a great place to suspend a poddy mullet underneath a float and target bream and dusky flathead.

16.17   PENGUIN HEAD

Situated at the northern end of Warrain Beach is a small headland called Penguin Head. This rock platform will produce bream, Australian salmon, tailor, drummer, luderick, groper and silver trevally. Try using cunje, peeled prawns, half and whole pilchards and squid for bait.

MAP 17 SHOALHAVEN UPSTREAM OF NOWRA BRIDGE

The headwaters of the Shoalhaven is a fast flowing stream with a reasonable population of rainbow and brown trout, freshwater blackfish and some native freshwater fish species.

There is now a dam at Talowa that was built in the 70s near the Kangaroo River. In these upper reaches below the dam the river is fresh water and free from tidal influence. As it makes its way through pastoral lands it becomes a brackish tidal estuary well before it reaches the township of Nowra.

17.1   PETE'S STRETCH

Many years ago a mate of mine (Dick) owned a place on this stretch of the upper Shoalhaven River and we use to fish from the shore here. We managed to catch bream, dusky flathead, Australian bass, mullet and mulloway. At the time Dick had a dog called Pete who use to catch very large eels while duck diving this stretch of shoreline. Hench the name Pete's Stretch.

This stretch of shoreline is just upstream from the bridge at Nowra on the northern side of the river. Great place to fish for bream and flathead.

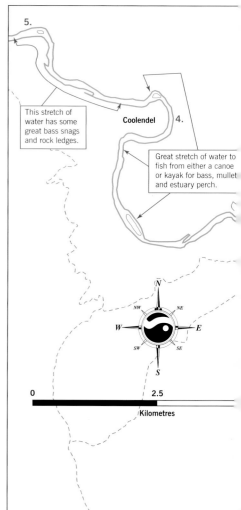

This stretch of water has some great bass snags and rock ledges.

Coolendel

Great stretch of water to fish from either a canoe or kayak for bass, mullet and estuary perch.

0   2.5
Kilometres

17.2 BUNDANON

The section of the Shoalhaven River which is not far from the art gallery at Bundanon is tidal and saline, so you can still catch all the saltwater species of fish such as bream, flathead, mullet and bass. You could head further up river to chase after the most popular river sport fish, the mighty bass. Perch and carp also inhabit the waters.

17.3 GRADY'S RIVERSIDE RETREAT

The section of the Shoalhaven River in front of Grady's Riverside Retreat is also tidal and saline, so all the saltwater species of fish such as bream, flathead and mullet are still able to be caught. Once again you could head further up river to chase after the most popular river sport fish, the mighty bass. You can also target perch and carp in these waters.

17.4 COOLENDEL

The more serious anglers are attracted to the upper reaches of the Shoalhaven River around Coolendel as it offers some of the best Australian bass fishing to be found. As one of Australia's most truly outstanding freshwater sports fish, bass respond to all methods of angling. Bass will respond to angling methods used by trout fishermen. This species has become extremely popular amongst the angling community especially in inland dams where it may be stocked by fishery departments and local angling groups.

LEFT: Dusky flathead can be caught upstream of the bridge at Nowra.

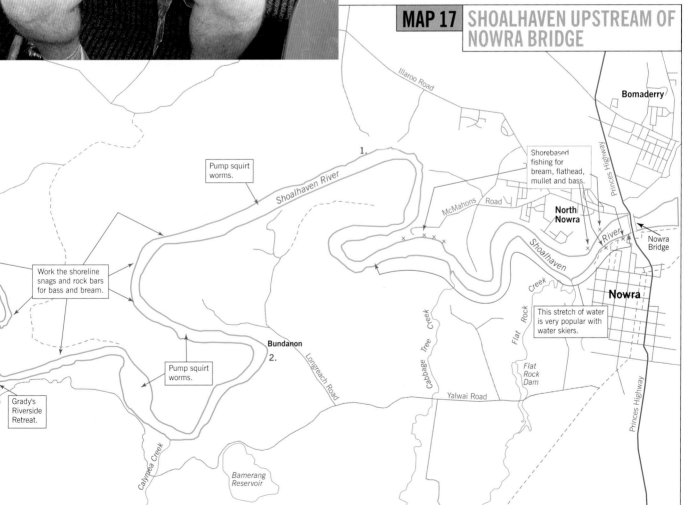

MAP 17 SHOALHAVEN UPSTREAM OF NOWRA BRIDGE

Bomaderry

Pump squirt worms.

Shoalhaven River

Shorebased fishing for bream, flathead, mullet and bass.

McMahons Road

North Nowra

Nowra Bridge

Work the shoreline snags and rock bars for bass and bream.

Flat Rock Creek

This stretch of water is very popular with water skiers.

Nowra

Pump squirt worms.

Bundanon
2.

Longreach Road

Cabbage Tree Creek

Flat Rock Dam

3.

Grady's Riverside Retreat.

Calymea Creek

Yalwai Road

Princes Highway

Bamerang Reservoir

Most bass specialists use small to medium sized cast floating lures, although trolling is effective at times. Surface lures are especially effective on bass, although a degree of finesse is usually required. With all lures, when fishing for bass, it is usually best to allow the lure to float on the surface for some time before beginning the retrieve. Occasionally pausing during the retrieve is also often effective.

Fly is effective in many areas, but the best natural bass waters are often heavily over grown and a degree of skill is required if one is not to become hopelessly tangled in the overhanging vegetation.

Coolendel is an idyllic setting of 127 acres located on the beautiful Shoalhaven River 30 kilometres west of Nowra. You can enjoy 2.5 kilometres river frontage with fresh water swimming and rapids for canoeing & liloing.

17.5   TALLOWA DAM

Tallowa Dam is a major part of the Shoalhaven water scheme and is situated at the junction of the Kangaroo and Shoalhaven Rivers, approximately 23 kilometres from the picturesque Kangaroo Valley township. Tallowa Dam supplements the Sydney water supply.

Adam Ford with a beautifully conditioned Australian bass.

MAP 18 JERVIS BAY —
BEECROFT HEAD TO SUMMER CLOUD BAY

Jervis Bay (plus Currarong, Callala Beach, Callala Bay, Myola, Vincentia and Hyams Beach). An area of brilliant white sands and pleasant bushwalking.

Located about 170 km from Sydney, Jervis Bay is both an inlet and the basis of the uniquely beautiful Booderee National Park which is a popular holiday destination.

Before I go on I will let you know that Jervis Bay is a marine reserve and there are a number of ZONES in the park. They are Sanctuary, Habital Protection, General Use, Special Purpose and Commonwealth. I would suggest that you get a copy of the Jervis Bay Marine Park brochure and familiarize your self with it.

The bay itself is approximately15km long and 10km wide. It is a spacious natural harbour sheltered by headlands of forest and heath land which jut out leaving a relatively narrow entrance. With a depth of 27 metres it is thought to be the deepest sheltered harbour in Australia. The waters are remarkably beautiful and range in hue from aquamarine to a deep blue. There are lakes and estuaries, historic sites, high sandy ridges, a coastline of coves, majestic cliffs up to 135 metres, and beaches noted for their length and the remarkable whiteness of their sands.

Whalers from Twofold Bay began to frequent Jervis Bay in the 1790s using it for anchorage. In 1801 naturalist and explorer George Caley arrived aboard Lieutenant James Grant's "Lady Nelson" and between them they made favourable reports of the flora, fauna and safety of the harbour.

The combination of projecting headlands, steep cliffs, rocky shoreline, currents and strong easterly winds proved a hazard to sailing vessels. Cape St George Lighthouse was constructed in 1860. However it was erected at the wrong spot, several kilometres north of Cape St George. As a result it was imperceptible to ships coming from the south and, ironically, proved a navigational hazard by day.

Four km south of Huskisson and just east off Jervis Bay Road is the small resort town of Vincentia. It was originally South Huskisson but was renamed in 1952 after John Jervis, after whom

High speed spinning for pelagics off the rocks as the sun rises in the east. Is there nothing better?

Jervis Bay was named, who was also the Earl of St Vincent. Vincentia is a typical holiday town. There are the usual modern facilities, long beaches and the waters are good for fishing, windsurfing, sailing and diving.

The first left turn off Elizabeth Drive is Holden Street which will take you out to the Bay and a concrete boat ramp. Hyams Beach is a quiet village which claims to have the whitest sand in the world. There is a concrete boat ramp off Cyrus Street into the Bay. Hyams Beach is also a recommended diving spot, at least at high tide. From the boat ramp swim out due east for 100 metres. There are a number of shallow reefs in 8–10 metres of water and a variety of temperate marine life. The site is not suitable during easterly swells or north-easterly winds.

Continue down to the end of Cave Beach Road (it is unsealed

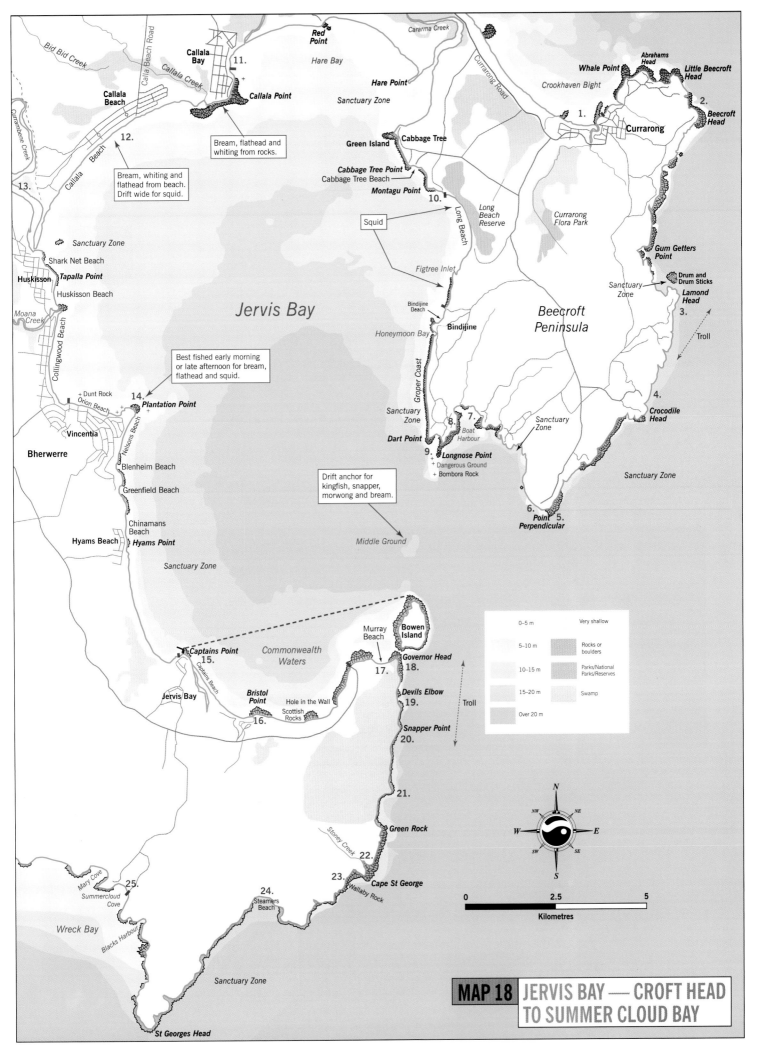

Bid Bid Creek

Calla Beach Road

Callala Creek

Callala Bay

11.

Red Point

Cararma Creek

Currarong Road

Whale Point

Abrahams Head

Little Beecroft Head

Crookhaven Bight

1.

2.

Beecroft Head

Currarong

Hare Bay

Hare Point

Sanctuary Zone

Callala Beach

Callala Point

Callala Beach

12.

Bream, flathead and whiting from rocks.

13.

Bream, whiting and flathead from beach. Drift wide for squid.

Currambene Creek

Green Island

Cabbage Tree

Cabbage Tree Point

Cabbage Tree Beach

Montagu Point

10.

Long Beach

Long Beach Reserve

Currarong Flora Park

Beecroft Peninsula

Gum Getters Point

Drum and Drum Sticks

Sanctuary Zone

Lamond Head

3.

Troll

Squid

Figtree Inlet

Jervis Bay

Sanctuary Zone

Shark Net Beach

Huskisson

Tapalla Point

Huskisson Beach

Moana Creek

Collingwood Beach

Best fished early morning or late afternoon for bream, flathead and squid.

Bindijine Beach

Bindijine

Honeymoon Bay

Groper Coast

Sanctuary Zone

4.

Crocodile Head

14.

Plantation Point

Dunt Rock

Orion Beach

Nelsons Beach

Vincentia

Bherwerre

Blenheim Beach

Greenfield Beach

Chinamans Beach

Hyams Beach

Hyams Point

Sanctuary Zone

Dart Point

8. **7.**

Boat Harbour

9. Longnose Point

Dangerous Ground

Bombora Rock

Sanctuary Zone

Sanctuary Zone

6. **5.**

Point Perpendicular

Drift anchor for kingfish, snapper, morwong and bream.

Middle Ground

Commonwealth Waters

Captains Point

15.

Captains Beach

Jervis Bay

Murray Beach

Bowen Island

Governor Head

18.

Bristol Point

16.

Hole in the Wall

Scottish Rocks

17.

Devils Elbow

19.

Troll

Snapper Point

20.

21.

Green Rock

Storey Creek

22.

23.

Cape St George

Mary Cove

25.

Summercloud Cove

24.

Steamers Beach

Wallaby Rock

Wreck Bay

Blacks Harbour

Sanctuary Zone

St Georges Head

	0–5 m	Very shallow
	5–10 m	Rocks or boulders
	10–15 m	Parks/National Parks/Reserves
	15–20 m	Swamp
	Over 20 m	

N
NW *NE*
W *E*
SW *SE*
S

0   2.5   5

Kilometres

MAP 18   **JERVIS BAY — CROFT HEAD TO SUMMER CLOUD BAY**

beyond the gardens) to the car park. A trail will take you the 300 m through coastal scrub to the beautifully-situated Cave Beach campsite which offers toilets, picnic facilities, barbecues and cold showers. From here you can either continue south to the beach, ideal for fishing and swimming, or head west through some rainforest to Bherwerre Beach where there are views to the south, and west, to the mangroves and swamps on the shoreline of St Georges Basin. Both Cave and Bherwerre are recommended surfing locations.

If you want a longer walk there is a fire trail which heads south-west from the road through tall blackbutt forest, coastal tea-tree and revegetated dunes down to Bherwerre Beach (1.9 km). There is a 200 m detour that heads east from the fire trail to Ryans Swamp, full of egrets, ibises, swamp hens and herons when flooded.

18.1   HONEYCOMBE BAY

This beach is protected in any wind that is coming from a southerly direction. It can be fished for bream, whiting, garfish and mullet. Fish as light as possible and with long leaders. Beach and blood worms, pink nippers and strips of mullet are the go for bait. Currarong, in Crookhaven Bight at the northernmost point of the Beecroft Peninsula, has a beautiful beach. There is also safe swimming for children at Currarong Creek. The fishing is reputedly excellent and there are two boat ramps: a concrete one on Warrain Crescent and a natural ramp across the sand into the ocean on Yalwal Street.

18.2   BEECROFT POINT

It is a bit of a trek out to this point from the caravan park, but it can be worth it. Bream, silver trevally, luderick, drummer, Australian salmon and tailor can be caught here on either side of the high tide. Whole or half pilchards, peeled prawns, pink nippers, cunje and strips of either tuna or mullet for bait. To get the best results you will need to take in some berley with you. This point is also a great place to high speed spin and chuck plastics for pelagics.

The Beecroft Peninsula is a beautiful and historic area with a diverse array of native flowers and wildlife. Bushwalking, fishing and camping are available at Honeymoon Bay on the western perimeter of the promontory, though on weekends and school holidays only. Unfortunately the peninsula is also used as a weapons range and so is subject to closure at short notice, making visits more problematic. However, it is well worth the effort. Telephone the Rangers Office about public access and camping (02 4448 3411 or 02 4448 3177).

18.3   NEVER FAIL

This can be a very dangerous spot to fish, so plenty of care will need to be taken when fishing. I would suggest that you let someone know that you are going here and when you are expecting to return. Great to fish for drummer, bream, snapper, pelagics and luderick.

18.4   CROCIDILE HEAD NORTH

This is a place where you can either high speed spin or live bait for kingfish, tuna, marlin and other pelagics, but it would have to be one of the most dangerous places on the peninsular to fish. A number of anglers have lost their lives trying to get to this spot. Try fishing the area from a boat.

18.5   POINT PERPENDICULAR

Deep water and high cliffs are found here and it is mainly a boat fishing area for tuna, kingfish, snapper and tailor. Extremely dangerous in a southerly swell.

They may only be small (rats) kingfish, but this young angler reckons it's the best fun he has had while fishing.

18.6 THE TUBES

There are remnants of old torpedo tubes that mark the sight of some extraordinary big fish captures of marlin tuna and kingfish. You can catch your slimy mackerel, yellowtail and bonito here for live bait. This spot can become very crowded when the fish are on the chew and this is due to the fact that the oceanic blue water currents will sweep right up against the rocks.

18.7 BOAT HARBOUR

Fish off the beach and the corner of the rocks for bream, whiting and the odd Australian salmon and tailor. Best baits I have found to use are beach and blood worms, plus pink nippers

18.8 TARGET BEACH

You will need to check whether you are allowed to go here as this area is part of the Naval bombing range and can be off limits at times. Bream, whiting, tailor, drummer, Australian salmon and luderick can be caught while fishing here.

18.9 DART POINT TO TARGET BEACH

Snapper, drummer, bream, silver trevally and luderick can be caught here. You could always berley up some yellowtail, mullet and garfish and try for a jewfish, tuna or kingfish that frequent the area as well. Pike and long tom can also be caught, but they can be a pest when you are targeting other fish species.

18.10 LONG BEACH

Try drifting off the beach here for squid, mullet, whiting, bream and sand flathead. You could also try trolling a couple of deep diving lures or skirted lures as well.

Troll the washes off Jervis Bay for Watson Leaping bonito.

18.11 NORTH CALLALA BEACH

This area features beaches perfect for swimming, sailing, snorkeling or just lazing about. There are concrete boat ramps at both Myola (Beach St, facing into the Creek) and Callala Bay. Bream, flathead, flounder, whiting and squid can be caught here on a rising tide. Best baits for me have been live prawns, nippers and beach worms. You could also try using strips of tuna or mullet.

18.12 SOUTH CALLALA

Again bream, whiting, flathead, flounder and squid can be caught here. Very similar to North Callala Beach. You could also try fishing the entrance to Currumbene Creek on a run-out tide. There have been a few large dusky flathead caught by those anglers who have been using live poddy mullet and small yellowtail.

18.13 CURRUMBENE CREEK

Just remember that part of this small and very clear at times creek has a sanctuary zone within it. Good place to try for squirt worms and pink nippers on a failing tide.

You can also try for poddy mullet and garfish on a rising tide.

18.14 LAMBS POINT

Whiting, bream, dusky flathead and squid can be caught here. Try fishing on a rising tide and just before the sun sets for the best results.

18.15 CAPTAINS POINT

Fish the breaking water for bream and luderick. There are schools of tailor, whiting and silver trevally during autumn and winter. Jewfish have been taken at night on whole squid and fillets of pike.

18.16 GREEN PATCH

Green Patch has a popular and beautiful camping ground accommodating caravans as well as tents. There are picnic tables, good barbecue facilities, toilets, hot showers but no power, an excellent sheltered beach and, best of all, hundreds of tame rosellas. The birdlife here is prolific, the flora is diverse, there are dolphins and penguins to be seen in the bay and kangaroos about the campsite. The maximum permissible stay is three weeks.

18.17 MURRAY'S BEACH

Beyond Green Patch, along Jervis Bay Road, several short walking trails lead to Scottish Rocks and the Hole in the Wall. At its end is Murray's Beach, recognised as a highlight of the reserve. From the large car park you walk to the shore, only to find a boat ramp and a small beach with rocky outcrops. If you are disappointed don't worry. This is not Murray's Beach. That lies a short 1.4 kilometre walk away around a rocky point and it is as beautiful as everyone suggests. A walking trail will take you on to Governor Head with its sandstone cliffs towering 90–120 metres above the waves. The trail continues south, as coastal scrub gives way to heath land, down to the end of Stony Creek Road then back north again to Murray's

Beach. The cliffs here, with their coloured sandstone layers, extend all the way down the eastern coast of the peninsula and around to St George Head on the southern side of the promontory.

Both Green Patch and Murray's Beach boat ramp are recommended locations for diving. Snorkeling spots are abundant. There are shallow and deep-water rock reefs, sand zones, sea grass meadows, silty sand-flats, platforms and caves to explore.

18.18   BLACK HOLE

Very good breaming spot. Fish a couple of hours either side of the top of the tide for the best results. Make sure that you take some berley with you.

18.19   DEVILS ELBOW

This can be another one of those very dangerous spots to fish in the bay, but it does produce good catches of bream, drummer, luderick and tailor on a rising and falling tide.

18.20   THE CAVES

This site is situated in between Devil's Elbow and the Pimple and is mainly considered as a boat spot for snapper, tailor, bream, tarwhine and reef leatherjackets.

18.21   THE OLD LIGHT

Try here for bream, drummer, luderick and groper. While fishing, you will need to watch the weather and the swell as it can come up very quickly. Make sure that you berley while fishing here.

18.22   STONEY CREEK

Many of the locals will come here to target luderick a couple of hours either side of the top of the tide.

18.23   WALLABY ROCK

Wallaby Rock is a top local spot for bream, drummer, luderick tailor and silver trevally.

18.24   STEAMERS BEACH

It may be a bloody long walk into Steamers Beach, but I haven't had it let me down yet. Everything I have caught here has been big. Tailor to two kilos, Australian salmon to four kilos, bream and luderick to a kilo and some of the drummer and groper I have tangled with here I have not been able to land

18.25   SUMMERCLOUD BAY

Just east of Summercloud Bay is Wreck Bay where there are a series of sandy bays with sheltered beaches. This area is accessible by taking Wreck Bay Road which heads south from Jervis Bay Road 2 km east of the Cave Beach Road turnoff. There is a path which turns off to the left before the 87 hectare Aboriginal settlement and then heads south again towards secluded Summercloud Bay, a pretty little cove that has a ramp, toilets, picnic tables, barbecues drinking water and beautiful beaches set against a backdrop of blackbutt forest.

The rock platform is popular with snorkelers. Both Summercloud Bay and Shelley's Point to the east are popular surfing spots.

MAP 19 SHOALHAVEN TO JERVIS BAY
— OFFSHORE GPS POINTS

19.1   NOWRA HILL
S 34 53 170   E 150 48 590

15 fathoms and 3 to 4 nautical miles out from the entrance to the Shoalhaven River. Jewfish, snapper, morwong, sweep, pig fish, kingfish and flathead around the sandy edge of the reef.

19.2   THE MUD
S 34 55 930   E 150 54 470

This area varies in depth from 20 to 25 fathoms and is 8 to 9 nautical miles from Greenwell Point. It fishes well for kingfish, snapper, jewfish and silver trevally.

19.3   THE EDGE
S 34 56 800   E 150 55 480

Fish here for all reef species. Best fished on a rising tide. 15 fathom deep. A mixture of reef, broken shale and sandy bottom.

19.4   THE LAKE
S 34 57 900   E 150 47 940

A great place to drift for flathead. Snapper, silver trevally and tailor can be caught here as well while on the drift.

Try for yellowfin tuna while fishing the Drumsticks Canyon.

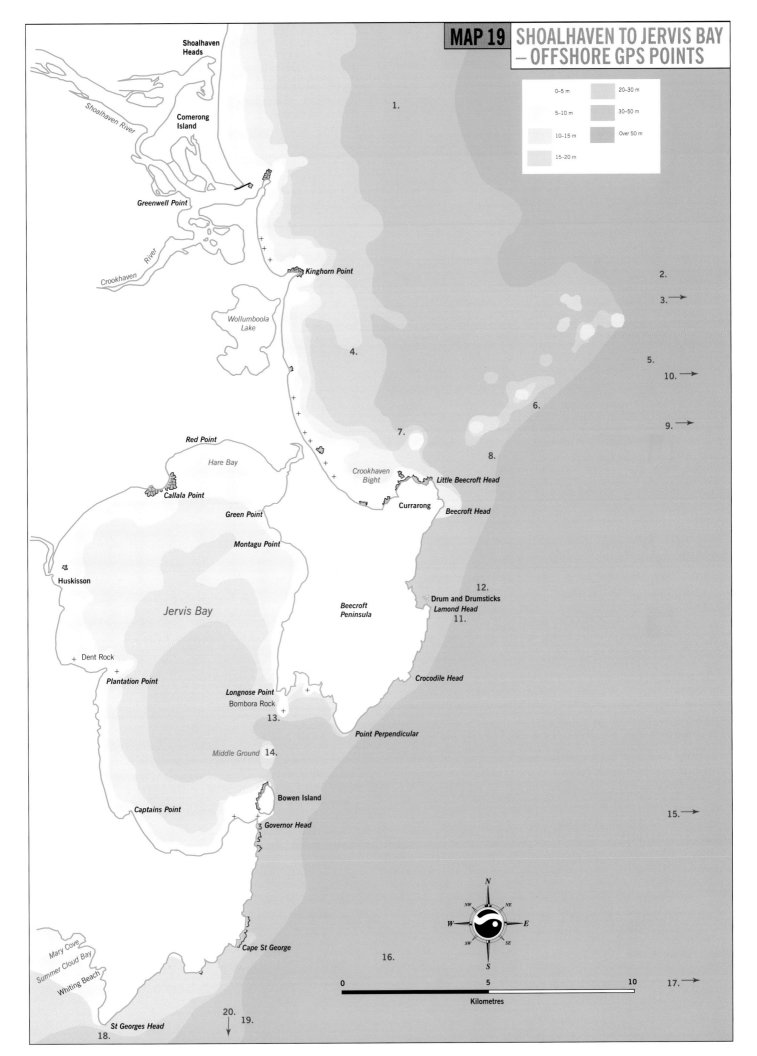

MAP 19 SHOALHAVEN TO JERVIS BAY
— OFFSHORE GPS POINTS

0–5 m
5–10 m
10–15 m
15–20 m
20–30 m
30–50 m
Over 50 m

Shoalhaven
Heads

Shoalhaven River

Comerong
Island

Greenwell Point

Crookhaven River

1.

Kinghorn Point

Wollumboola
Lake

2.

3. →

4.

5.

10. →

6.

9. →

7.

8.

Red Point

Hare Bay

Crookhaven
Bight

Little Beecroft Head

Callala Point

Currarong

Beecroft Head

Green Point

Montagu Point

Huskisson

12.

Drum and Drumsticks

Lamond Head

11.

Jervis Bay

Beecroft
Peninsula

Dent Rock

Crocodile Head

Plantation Point

Longnose Point

Bombora Rock

13.

Point Perpendicular

Middle Ground 14.

Captains Point

Bowen Island

Governor Head

15. →

N

NW   NE

W   E

SW   SE

S

Mary Cove

Summer Cloud Bay

Whiting Beach

Cape St George

16.

0   5   10

Kilometres

17. →

20. 19.

St Georges Head

18.

Don't forget to try jigging for kingfish on the close inshore reefs off the Shoalhaven Shire.

19.5   SHALLOWS
S 34 58 610   E 150 53 030

10 fathoms deep and fish here for most reef species. Also worth trolling the area for tailor, Australian salmon and kingfish.

19.6   THE HUMPS
S 34 59 170   E 150 51 770

20 fathoms deep and fishes well for kingfish, snapper, sweep, leatherjackets, jewfish and tuna. Try trolling here as well.

19.7   CURRARRONG BOMBIE
S 34 59 390   E 150 49 150

Care needs to be taken when fishing here as the depth is only 5 to 6 fathoms. Fishes well for snapper, leatherjackets, silver trevally, bream, john dory, trags, jewfish and the odd kingfish.

19.8   BEECROFT HEAD
S 35 00 540   E 150 51 650

25 fathoms. 8 to 9 nautical miles from Greenwell Point. 10 nautical miles from Murray's Beach boat ramp. Mainly snapper, morwong and leatherjackets.

19.9   THE BANKS WIDE
S 35 00 910   E 151 03 740

100 fathoms. 18 nautical miles from Greenwell Point. Fishes well for albacore, marlin, tuna and kingfish. You can also target snapper here as well.

19.10   BLOCK AND CHEESE
S 34 58 530   E 150 59 160

13 nautical miles from Murray's Beach. Fairly large area of reef that fishes very well for most reef species, snapper, sea perch, morwong and nannygai.

19.11   DRUM AND DRUMSTICKS
S 35 02 820   E 150 50 450

This is an excellent spot for kingfish, snapper, bream, silver trevally. It is 11 nautical miles from the Shoalhaven, 7 nautical miles from Murray's Beach and 16 nautical miles from Huskisson. There is a good drop off on the eastern side of the reef where you can anchor and berley on a falling tide.

19.12   DRUM AND DRUMSTICKS EAST
S 35 02 820   E 150 52 400

This end of the reef is between 1.7 to 2 nautical miles east of Drum and Drumsticks. Fish here for kingfish, bream, snapper, leatherjackets and morwong.

19.13   LONGNOSE POINT BOMBIE
S 35 05 100   E 150 46 450

3 nautical miles from Murray's Beach and 7.5 nautical miles from Huskisson. Fishes very well for snapper, Australian salmon, tailor, kingfish, bream and silver trevally.

19.14   MIDDLE GROUND
S 35 06 100   E 150 46 200

7.5 nautical miles from Huskisson. A good spot to drift for flathead and bream, but you can also catch tuna, kingfish, bonito and silver trevally here.

19.15   DRUMSTICKS CANYON
S 35 08 300   E 151 00 780

180 fathoms deep and fishes well for marlin, kingfish and tuna. 12 nautical miles from the Murray's Beach boat ramp and 21 nautical miles from Huskisson

19.16   STONEY CREEK
S 35 10 690   E 150 48 390

40 fathoms deep. Kingfish, snapper, black marlin are targeted here throughout the year. 3 nautical miles from the ramp at Murray's Beach and 12 nautical miles from Huskisson.

19.17   JB CANYONS 120 FATHOMS
S 35 11 960   E 150 58 600

Yellowfin, albacore, black, striped and blue marlin, sharks and kingfish can be targeted here. Bottom bash for hapuka, blue eye, trevalla and broadbill. 12 to 13 nautical miles from Murray's Beach, 22 to 23 nautical miles from Huskisson and 25 nautical miles from Shoalhaven Heads.

19.18   ST GEORGE'S DROP-OFF
S 35 12 296   E 150 41 768

General reef fishing in 43 to 50 fathoms of water.

19.19   90 METRE MARK
S 35 12 667   E 150 44 612

45 fathoms for snapper, morwong, kingfish and leatherjackets.

19.20   100 METRE MARK
S 35 13 350   E 150 43 730

50 fathoms for snapper, morwong, kingfish and leatherjackets.

BOAT RAMPS NORTH OF THE SHOALHAVEN RIVER TO WARRAIN BEACH AT CURRARONG

Name	Make	Condition	No of Lanes	Wash Down	Lights	Fish Clean	BBQ	Toilets
Map 16	**Shoalhaven River Entrance to Nowra Bridge**							
Haiser Road Greenwell Point	Concrete	Good	1	Yes	Yes	Yes	No	Yes
West Street Greenwell Point	Concrete	Good	1	No	Yes	No	No	No
Adelaide Street Greenwell Point	Concrete	Poor	1	Yes	Yes	No	Yes	Yes
Broughton Creek Shoalhaven	Gravel	Good	1	No	No	No	No	No
Greys Beach	Concrete	Excellent	3	Yes	Yes	Yes	No	Yes
Otranto Ave Orient Point	Concrete	Good	1	No	Yes	No	No	Yes
Hay Avenue Shoalhaven Heads	Concrete	Good	1	No	No	Yes	No	No
River Road Shoalhaven Heads	Concrete	Good	1	Yes	Yes	Yes	Yes	Yes
Prince Edward Ave Crookhaven Heads	Concrete	Good	2	Yes	Yes	Yes	No	Yes
Map 17	**Shoalhaven upstream of Nowra Bridge**							
Wharf Road Nowra	Concrete	Good	1	No	Yes	No	No	Yes
Map 18	**Jervis Bay—Beecroft Head to Summer Cloud Bay**							
Murray Beach Jervis Bay Road Jervis Bay	Concrete	Good	1	No	Yes	Yes	No	Yes
Catherine Street Myola	Concrete	Good	1	No	No	No	No	Yes
Cyrus Street Hyams Beach Jervis Bay	Sand	Poor	1	No	No	No	No	Yes
Watt Street Callala Bay	Concrete	Good	1	Yes	Yes	Yes	Yes	Yes
Vincentia Jervis Bay	Rock	Poor	1	No	No	No	Yes	Yes

TACKLE SHOPS NORTH OF THE SHOALHAVEN RIVER TO WARRAIN BEACH AT CURRARONG

MCCALLUM SPORTS
47 Kinghorn Street Nowra
PHONE: (02) 4421 2418

ANGLERS REST CARAVAN PARK
Greenwell Point Rd Greenwell Point
PHONE: (02) 4447 1207

CULBURRA BAIT AND TACKLE
171 Prince Edward Ave Culburra
PHONE: (02) 4447 2087

JERVIS BAY TACKLE
9 Nowra Street Huskisson
PHONE: 0422 429385

CHAPTER 4
SUSSEX INLET
St Georges Basin to Lake Conjola

For many years this stretch of the south coast has been a secret to only the people who used to visit here regularly. The small townships of Lake Conjola, Sussex Inlet and St Georges Basin are tucked away off the main highway and were by passed by many people who were heading south to places like Ulladulla, Burrill Lake and Batemans Bay. Not a lot has changed at these places, unless you count the increase in new homes, younger families taking up residence, mobile homes and more tourists.

One of the things that I have found, is that even though the fishing pressure has increased in the area, the fishing is as great as it has ever been when I have been down there, but maybe some of the locals will not agree with this.

Since the banning of professional fishing in St Georges Basin and the installation of a number of artificial reefs the basin has improved heaps. I usually visit this stretch of coastline at least 8 times a year and have caught large dusky flathead, sand whiting as thick as your wrist, jewfish to 8 kilos, blue swimmer crabs, dinner plate sized flounder and even a number of snapper and kingfish in the bay. All of which have been caught on either hard bodied lures or soft plastics.

One of the other places that are off the beaten track is the small township of Bendalong Point. Many years ago I use to surf here when the seas were very big and fish the same area after the seas had abated.

A four wheel drive vehicle is needed to reach a couple of the places I fish in this area.

MAP 20 ST GEORGES HEAD AND SOUTH TO MOLLYMOOK
– BEACH AND ROCK

St George's Head is at the southern end of the Booderee National Park and has many hidden fishing secrets that the adventurous angler can locate. There are places like Steamers Beach. A 2 km walk from the car park brings you to the top of the cliff at the western end of the beach. A steep 300 m descent gets you onto the sand. Further south are Cudmirrah, Manyana and Conjola Beaches.

Overnight accommodation is available at places like Bendalong, Lake Conjola, Narrawallee and Mollymook.

20.1 CAVES BEACH

I stumbled across Caves Beach many years ago when I was out looking for a surf with a couple of mates. There had been big seas running for four days and most of the spots we had gone to were blown out. Upon arriving at Caves Beach, we were not only confonted with surf, but huge schools of Australian salmon and tailor. It was a shame we didn't have our rods. Since then I have ventured back down to Caves Beach a few days after a big blow and have had a number of great sessions on Australian salmon and tailor. I have also picked up a few bream and whiting as well.

20.2 BHERWERRE BEACH

Bherwerre Beach is a long, south-facing ocean beach also approached from Cave Beach car park. Take the main trail from the car park to the camping area. On the western side of the camp area there is a trail that leads around Ryans Swamp to Bherwerre Beach.

20.3 CUDMIRRAH BEACH

Cudmirrah Beach is the surf beach for Sussex Inlet and a good one at that with waves averaging 1.6 m. The beach is 3 km long extending from the 60 m high sandstone headland and rocks at Sussex Inlet to the lee of the reef and sand spit on the north side of the usually closed mouth of Swan Lake. The beach is backed by active sand dunes extending a few hundred meters inland and to heights of 30 m. The only car access is to a small car park behind the Surf Club. The entire beach faces straight into the south east swell and has a high energy surf zone typified by strong rips. Up to 10 large rips usually dominate the beach, with the largest in the north and a permanent rip against the rocks. To the south slight protection in lee of the reef reduces wave height and rip intensity.

Tailor, Australian salmon, bream, whiting and jewfish can be caught along the beach. When you get there you can stop in the car park of the Surf Life Saving Club and view the various fish holding gutters and rips from here.

20.4 BERRARA

Apart from the usual surfing, swimming, fishing, canoeing, bushwalking, bicycle riding you could walk along the power pole track to Fisherman's Rock or you can walk along the bottom track from the Berrara Lagoon Reserve – as long as it hasn't been raining. Here you will find an excellent place to fish or picnic. The NPWS have provided picnic tables.

If you walk south along Berrara Beach to the rocky headland,

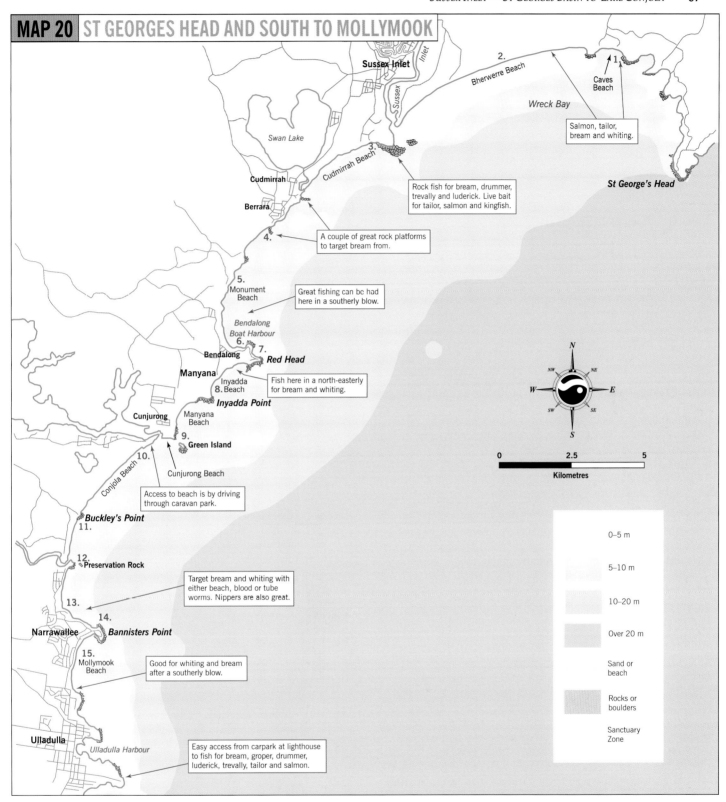

MAP 20   ST GEORGES HEAD AND SOUTH TO MOLLYMOOK

Sussex Inlet

Bherwerre Beach

Caves Beach

Wreck Bay

Salmon, tailor, bream and whiting.

Swan Lake

3.

St George's Head

Cudmirrah

Cudmirrah Beach

Berrara

Rock fish for bream, drummer, trevally and luderick. Live bait for tailor, salmon and kingfish.

4.

A couple of great rock platforms to target bream from.

5.
Monument Beach

Great fishing can be had here in a southerly blow.

Bendalong Boat Harbour

6.   7.

Bendalong   Red Head

Manyana

Inyadda
8. Beach

Fish here in a north-easterly for bream and whiting.

Inyadda Point

Cunjurong   Manyana Beach

9.   Green Island

10.

Cunjurong Beach

Conjola Beach

Access to beach is by driving through caravan park.

Buckley's Point
11.

12.
Preservation Rock

Target bream and whiting with either beach, blood or tube worms. Nippers are also great.

13.

14.

Narrawallee   Bannisters Point

15.
Mollymook Beach

Good for whiting and bream after a southerly blow.

Ulladulla   Ulladulla Harbour

Easy access from carpark at lighthouse to fish for bream, groper, drummer, luderick, trevally, tailor and salmon.

N
NW   NE
W   *E*
SW   SE
S

0   2.5   5
Kilometres

0–5 m

5–10 m

10–20 m

Over 20 m

Sand or beach

Rocks or boulders

Sanctuary Zone

and walk across the flat rocks, you will find the Mermaid Pool. A beautiful natural swimming pool in the rocks. Watch it at high tide as water can pour into Mermaid like a waterfall. If you don't feel like a swim, take some bread with you, sit up on the rocks and throw the bread in the pool and watch the fish feed.

20.5   MONUMENT BEACH

Bream and whiting are the main stay fish species that are targeted by anglers who fish this beach. You could have a throw at night for tailor and jewfish on a rising tide.

20.6   INSIDE BENDALONG

The small cove is officially known as Boat Harbour and is the traditional anchoring and launching spot for small boats to gain access to the sea. But like any ocean launching spot, you will need to take care of the seas. Fish this cove when the seas are running for drummer, whiting, bream and tailor on a rising tide.

20.7   BENDALONG POINT

About 11 km south of the Sussex Inlet turn off you will see a road sign directing you to the small township of Bendalong. Bendalong is about 12 km from the highway and the main beach is snugged away in behind a headland that protects it from the predominant south-easterly winds. When these winds are blowing you can fish this part of the headland and beach for drummer, bream, whiting and tailor.

20.8   INYADDA POINT

This small, but very productive point is nested in between Manyana and Inyadda Beaches and to get to here you will need to travel along Bendalong Road to Manyana. From here you can fish off Manyana, Inyadda and Cunjurong Beaches for whiting, bream and flathead. If beach fishing is not to your liking you can always try for drummer, luderick, bream and tailor off Inyadda and Cunjurong Points.

20.9   GREEN ISLAND

Outside the entrance of Lake Conjola is Green Island. It is separated from the land and a shallow sandy spit. Anglers can walk across to the island on the lower parts of the tide and fish for drummer, groper, bream, snapper and drummer. You will need to keep an eye on the tide as you don't want to be coming back across here when the water is chest deep.

20.10   CONJOLA BEACH

To get to Lake Conjola Beach you will need to turn off the Princes Highway just north of Ulladulla onto Lake Conjola Entrance Road and drive right to the end of it. This beach is a favoured place for anglers to target flathead, whiting, bream, tailor, mullet, Australian salmon and jewfish. Access to the beach is by driving through the caravan park near the entrance to the lake and parking in the car park. It is about a five to ten minute walk to the beach. Whole pilchards and garfish, strips of tuna and mullet, live beach and blood worms and live nippers are great baits for this beach.

20.11   BUCKLEY'S POINT

If you don't mind a bit of a walk, try heading south from the cark park at the entrance to Lake Conjola to Buckley's Point. Here you can fish for bream, whiting, drummer, tailor and the odd jewfish and shark.

20.12   PRESERVATION ROCK

Fish on the northern side of this point when the tide is falling and the nearby inlet is open to the sea for luderick, bream, flathead, whiting, tailor and the odd jewfish. Make sure that you have a small, but constant berley trail going for the best results.

20.13   NARRAWALLEE

Narrawallee has a gorgeous beach with the most inviting white sand. You can see the water colour change during various weather conditions and different times of the day. Narrawallee Beach is patrolled from October to April off season during weekends and the busy season daily. The patrols take place down at the southern end of the beach. If you visit our beach make sure you have sun protection with you and the appropriate clothing. During January keep a look out for blue bottles; these float in on the water on the NE winds.

Target, bream and whiting from this beach at high tide with pink nippers, beach and blood worms for the best results.

Narrawallee Inlet is located to the northern end of Narrawallee; you can access the inlet via Matron Porter Drive or Normandy Street which has the boat ramp access. If you intend using the inlet for fishing in a boat please take note of the tide or you may be carrying your boat back to the ramp at low tide.

Narrawallee Inlet is the perfect spot if you have young children as it's well protected and not too deep. Easy access for families, play area is also available plus, gas BBQ and tables placed around the reserve.

20.14   BANNISTERS POINT

Try fishing in the northern corner where the point meets Mollymook Beach for bream and whiting on a rising tide. Walk south to the southern rocks that provide a wide, flat access to deeper water. Care needs to be taken when fishing from here.

20.15   MOLLYMOOK BEACH

Mollymook became a popular weekend and holiday destination when it was subdivided for residential development in the mid 1960s. However the Ulladulla and Milton locals had long known about this beautiful beach below the golf course. Now Mollymook is part of the residential sprawl which extends north to Narrawallee. The beach retains much of its natural beauty with the golf course dominating the southern headland, and reserves surrounding the small central and northern creeks which flow across the beach during and after heavy rain.

The beach can be best accessed from the large car park around the surf club in the south and across the foreshore reserve along the northern half of the beach. The beach sweeps in a 2 km long broad east facing arc, between Bannisters Point in the north and the southern headland. A rock reef lies off the central portion of the beach, while in the south the headland and northward trending reef reduces waves to produce a continuous attached bar in front of the Surf Club.

Best beach fishing is up the beach in the rip holes, while the southern rocks provide a wide, flat access to deeper water.

Australian salmon can be caught during the middle of the day off the beach. Try using a bit of berley while you fish.

MAP 21 ST GEORGES BASIN

St Georges Basin is a significant coastal lake with a large shallow basin connected to the ocean by a narrow channel at the village of Sussex Inlet. This channel exits the basin at its southern shore. Wandandian Creek, the main tributary to the basin, forms a substantial fluvial delta at its entrance in the north-west corner of the lake. The towns of Sanctuary Point and St Georges Basin are located on the northern shore of the lake. Booderee National Park (under the authority of the Australian Capital Territory) borders the basin on its eastern edge. Large proportions of its catchment are modified.

You can target, dusky flathead, bream, whiting, jewfish, leatherjackets, mullet, snapper, tailor, kingfish, flounder, Australian bass and the odd estuary perch in the Basin.

21.1 WANDADIAN CREEK

If you have never been for a drive up this creek and you are into chasing bream, I would suggest that the next time that you visit St Georges Basin you take a look. There are plenty of snags, mangroves, mud slides, rock bars and drop offs where you can cast either a lure or a soft plastic. You are also in with a chance of getting whiting, dusky flathead, flounder, mullet and Australian bass.

21.2 PICNIC POINT

Try drifting the stretch of shoreline from Picnic to Bream Point. Here you can target bream, dusky flathead, whiting and the occasional snapper. Whitebait, half or whole pilchards, pink nippers, blood worms and strips of mullet, yellowtail and tuna are worth a go for bait.

21.3 SEPULCHRE ISLAND

Use your sounder to locate the many drop-offs and ledges that are around this island to target large dusky flathead with live poddy mullet, whitebait and small yellowtail. You could also try whole garfish and WA pilchards on a set of ganged hooks, or if you are not into bait and you prefer to use artificials, try jigging soft plastics and metal blades along the ledges and at the edges of the drop-offs.

Bream, whiting, leatherjackets, snapper, jewfish, tailor and the odd kingfish have been caught here on the run-out tide.

21.4 GARDEN ISLAND

The area around Garden Island is very similar to Sepulchre Island; it's just that the water depth is more. Bream, whiting, leatherjackets, snapper, jewfish, tailor, dusky flathead and the odd kingfish have been caught here on all tides. You could also try drifting the shallower areas, where the weed beds meet the sandy areas for whiting, bream and flathead on a rising tide. Both of these islands also have a few rocky points and rock bars that are covered with oysters. These areas are good for targeting bream on surface lures.

21.5 SWAN BAY

This bay is mostly very shallow and can fished two hours either side of the top of the tide for bream, flathead, flounder, and whiting. Not a bad place to put out a couple of witches hats for blue swimmer crabs. Also try anchoring in the deeper section of the front of the bay on a run-out tide for bream, whiting, flathead, jewfish and snapper. Berley is a must. You could also try prawning on the dark of the moon in the shallows during the summer months.

21.6 ONE TREE BAY

There is a small creek that flows into the end of this bay that is worth a shot during a very high, high tide for mullet, garfish and prawns. Work the edges of the weed beds on a run-out tide for bream, whiting and dusky flathead.

The author with a St George's Basin caught snapper.

21.7 KANAGROO POINT

The depth of the water does vary a fair bit here and is good for chasing jewfish, bream and dusky flathead. Blue swimmer crabs can also be targeted here as well.

21.8 SANCTUARY POINT

Try slow trolling lures along the shallow shoreline that is found here. If trolling is not your go you can work the same area with soft plastics, shallow and deep diving hard bodied lures. I have also caught a few massive whiting here on surface poppers. Troll out wider for tailor and the odd kingfish.

21.9 EROWAL BAY

Very shallow bay and is best fish about an hour either side of the top of the tide for bream, whiting, flathead, tailor and flounder. Concentrate on the sandy patches within the weed beds when chasing flathead.

21.10 CABBAGE TREE POINT

During a few flathead competitions that I have fished in the bay this is one of the spots that I have caught a number of dusky flathead on soft plastics. This stretch of shoreline is usually very consistent place to target dusky flathead. Bream, snapper, tailor and jewfish are also caught here.

21.11 THE SPIT

Good spot to either troll or cast lures for bream, dusky flathead and tailor.

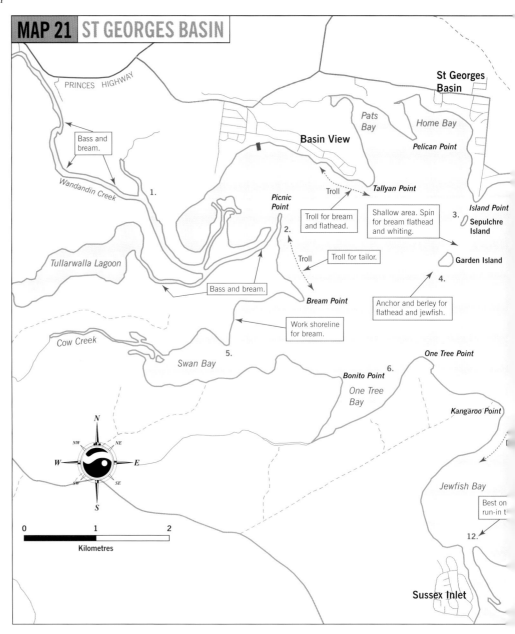

Since the artificial reefs have been put into the St Georges Basin near Sactuary Point, the average sizes and numbers of silver trevally have increased ten fold.

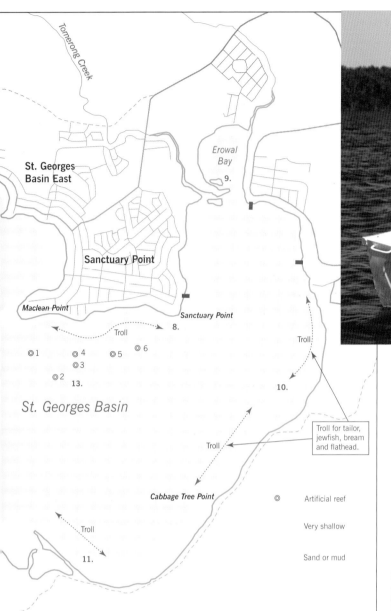

St. Georges Basin

Troll for tailor,
jewfish, bream
and flathead.

◎ Artificial reef

Very shallow

Sand or mud

ABOVE: A monster dusky
flathead that was caught
while fishing near Garden
Island in St Georges Basin.

RIGHT: Andrew McGovern
releasing a beautifully
condition dusky flathead.

BELOW: Cabbage Tree Point
produces dusky flathead on a
failing tide. Work the edge of
the weed beds.

21.12   SUSSEX INLET ENTRANCE

Just remember if you anchor here to fish the run-in tide, please keep
out of the way of other craft that will use this entrance. It can be a
very busy place. Berley for bream, dusky flathead, jewfish, mullet,
whiting and tailor on the run-in tide.

21.13   NSW FISHERIES ARTIFICAL REEFS

REEF 1	S 35 07 303	E 150 36 622
REEF 2	S 35 07 491	E 150 36 900
REEF 3	S 35 07 396	E 150 37 436
REEF 4	S 35 07 314	E 150 37 436
REEF 5	S 35 07 314	E 150 37 701
REEF 6	S 35 07 271	E 150 37 970

The artificial reefs are being constructed using existing 'Reef Ball'
technology. Reef balls are individual reef modules cast from a single
mould. The Reef Ball modules are a patented mould supplied by
the Reef Ball Development Group and made from a special mix of
concrete that enhances marine growth while withstanding saltwater
corrosion.

The Department is using 'Mini-Bay Reef Balls', which when
placed together on the bottom in varying numbers, form small
artificial reefs of different sizes. The individual reef ball modules
create habitat for marine fish, algae and crustaceans and can be
deployed, moved or retrieved if necessary.

You can target yellowtail, mullet, snapper, whiting, dusky
flathead, bream, flounder, crabs, kingfish and jewfish at this
artificial reef.

MAP 22 SUSSEX INLET

Sussex Inlet is about 50km south east of Nowra and is situated on the southern side of the beautiful waterways at the neck of St Georges Basin. The town itself seems surrounded by water and is sometimes referred to as an island getaway. Water sports are the most popular pastimes in the area with fishing being the most famous.

Fishing on the peaceful waters of St Georges Basin is a great way to unwind and the reason so many people return year after year. Boat hire is readily available. An Annual Family Fishing Carnival is held for a week each July and attracts many fishing enthusiasts who cast their lines in the hope of winning one of the many prizes. A variety of events are held including competitions for children. Beach fishing is also handy at nearby Cudmirrah and Bherwerre beaches.

Other activities you can enjoy on our waterways include snorkeling and scuba diving, sailing, windsurfing, canoeing and of course swimming and surfing.

Also available here are golfing and bowling. A local cinema and two licensed clubs will help keep you entertained during your stay. A wide variety of reserves and bush and beach walks will ensure you get a taste of our unspoilt natural environment. Accommodation in and around the town is offered by caravan parks and camping areas, cottages, cabins, units and motels.

22.1   ENTRANCE TO ST GEORGE'S BASIN

When you anchor here you will need to keep to either side of the waterway, as there are plenty of boats that travel up and down this stretch of water. I anchor my boat so that I can fish parallel to the weed beds for whiting, bream, flathead and luderick. If there are no boats anchored here you could try drifting this stretch of shoreline while casting out a few lures and soft plastics.

22.2   RIVER ROAD BRIDGE

Fish on either side of the bridge for bream, whiting, flathead and mullet. It doesn't seem to matter which tide it is, as long as there is some movement in the water. Berley for the best results and fish as light as possible. A very small ball sinker directly onto the bait would be a good rig to start with.

22.3   PHIL'S CORNER

One of the guys from work comes down to Sussex and fishes a lot for dusky flathead. Phil will either anchor here on the run-out tide and use live poddy mullet for bait or drift the same area and use soft plastics for the large dusky flathead that can be caught at times. Luderick will also frequent this stretch of water.

22.4   JACOBS DRIVE

Either anchor here or drift out with the tide for bream, whiting, flathead, mullet, crabs and luderick. You can cast a line or two from the shore.

22.5   SUSSEX INLET CANALS

When ever I am down this way with my boat I will work my way around these canals while casting either hard bodied lures, soft plastics and blades for bream, flathead, whiting, luderick and the odd tailor or two. If you have a boat that is fitted with an electric motor at the front it will make life easier when fishing these canals.

22.6   THE BEND

During the winter months luderick can be seen schooling up here along the weed beds, rock bars and mangroves. Dusky flathead will

ABOVE: How good are those blades? This TT Switch blade was worked slowly along the edge of the weed beds near the entrance to the St Georges Basin.

lay in wait for those poddy mullet during the summer months and bream can be targeted here during the autumn months.

22.7   RESERVE ROAD

Boat or shore fishing here for bream, flathead, whiting and luderick on the run-out tide. Best baits have been beach and blood worms, pink nippers, squirt worms and strip of fresh mullet.

22.8   CHRIS'S REACH

Many years ago I took my son (Chris) down to Sussex Inlet for a few days fishing. It was here that Chris caught bream while bait, hard bodied and lure fishing. We did also manage to catch a few dusky flathead and whiting as well.

22.9   ALAMEIN ROAD

Drift this area for mullet, garfish, luderick, bream, whiting, flounder, flathead and crabs on the run-out tide.

22.10   WHITING CORNER

Now, as the name suggests the last time I fished here I caught a number of large whiting. All of the fish were caught on beach worms that I had caught off Cudmirrah Beach. You can also try for flathead, mullet and bream as well.

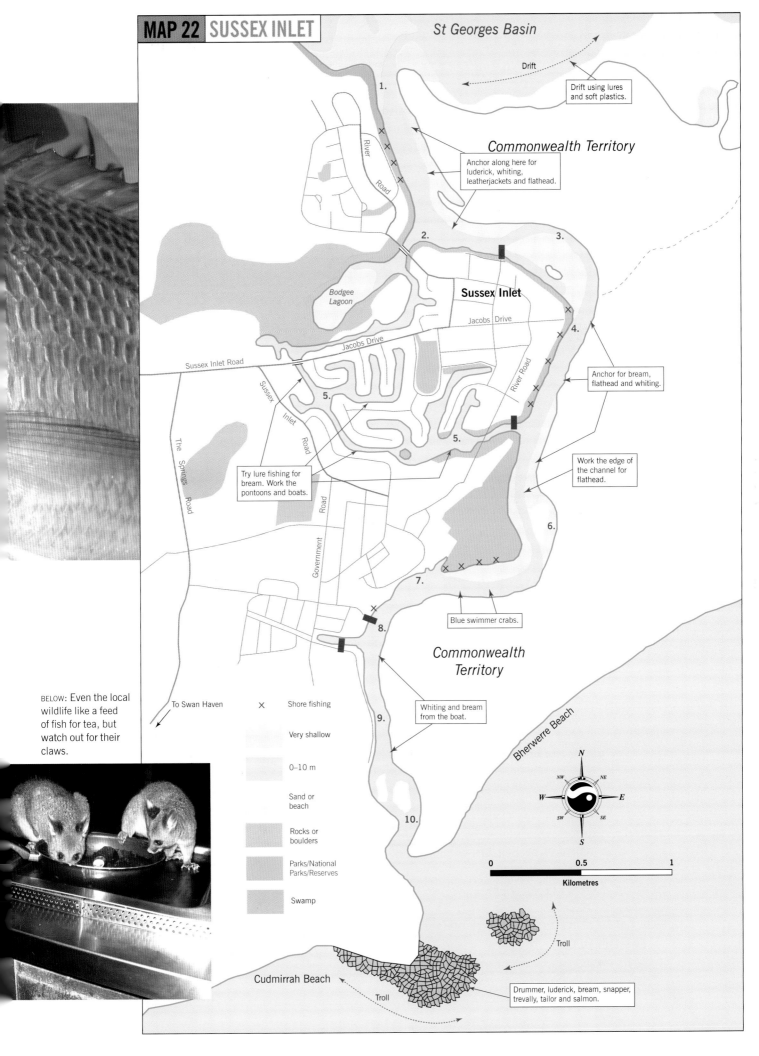

MAP 22 | SUSSEX INLET

St Georges Basin

Drift

Drift using lures and soft plastics.

1.

River Road

Commonwealth Territory

Anchor along here for luderick, whiting, leatherjackets and flathead.

2.

3.

Sussex Inlet

Bodgee Lagoon

Jacobs Drive

4.

Jacobs Drive

Sussex Inlet Road

Sussex Inlet Road

Anchor for bream, flathead and whiting.

5.

River Road

The Springs Road

5.

Work the edge of the channel for flathead.

Try lure fishing for bream. Work the pontoons and boats.

6.

Government Road

7.

Blue swimmer crabs.

8.

Commonwealth Territory

BELOW: Even the local wildlife like a feed of fish for tea, but watch out for their claws.

To Swan Haven

✕   Shore fishing

Very shallow

0–10 m

Sand or beach

Rocks or boulders

Parks/National Parks/Reserves

Swamp

Whiting and bream from the boat.

9.

Bherwerre Beach

N
NW   NE
W   E
SW   SE
S

10.

0   0.5   1
Kilometres

Troll

Cudmirrah Beach

Troll

Drummer, luderick, bream, snapper, trevally, tailor and salmon.

MAP 23 LAKE CONJOLA

Lake Conjola is situated just north of Ulladulla right on the coast. The lake empties into the Tasman Sea and most of the times are crystal clear. The lower section of the lake has extensive sand flats which are great for large dusky flathead, whiting and bream. This is the largest lake in the area almost permanently open to the sea. However the sea entrance in dangerous and not navigable. Three boat ramps around the lake provide access for small and large boats. It is also one of the most beautiful lakes in the state. Best fishing is between spring and autumn. There are many species of fish in the lake so fish with live bait, which is your best bet to catch flathead, snapper and jewfish.

Also commonly caught in the lake are blue swimmer crabs, leatherjackets, flounder, tailor, garfish, mullet, prawns and luderick. You can also target Australian salmon, tailor, bream, whiting and jewfish off the beach out in front of the caravan park.

The upper reaches of the lake consists mainly of shallow ribbon weed beds, sandy patches and the odd rocky shoreline, but this shouldn't deter you from fishing or prawning in this area.

23.1 FISHERMAN'S PARADISE

Fisherman's Paradise is mainly a very shallow weed flats that is not fished as much as the other areas of the lake. Definitely worth a shot on those windy days for bream, flathead, luderick and mullet. There are also a number of places that you can successfully fish from the shore at high tide.

23.2 SUNNY HILL

Work those lures and soft plastics along the edges of the weed beds for bream and dusky flathead during the warmer months of the year. During the colder months I would switch to live poddy mullet and white bait.

23.3 MELLA MELLA BAY

Up in the back reaches of this bay there are a couple of spots that you can try pumping for pink nippers and squirt worms. Try fishing the edges of the weed beds for luderick, bream, whiting and the odd dusky flathead. You could also try trolling those soft plastics and hard bodied lures along the edge of the weed beds. Tailor can also be caught up here at time during the winter months.

23.4 CUNNDENARRAH ARM

This arm has fairly deep water that rises up to the shoreline fairly quickly. Fish the edges for bream dusky flathead, blue swimmer crabs, luderick and leatherjackets. Garfish and mullet can also be berleyed up here on a rising tide. This is also a good place to work those hard bodied lures and soft plastics for bream. Pink nippers and squirt worms can be pumped in the end of the bay at low tide.

23.5 SANDY POINT

Try trolling for tailor from Sandy Point to Kilarney during May through to July. Deep diving minnows and small skirted lures are worth a shot here. You could also drift from point to point and work those soft plastics for dusky flathead, but you will need to watch out for water skiers.

23.6 STATION POINT

The rocky foreshore that is found here will produce tailor, bream, whiting, dusky flathead, leatherjackets and luderick on either a rising or falling tide.

ABOVE: Dusky flathead of this size will test out even the best of anglers. Try downsizing your gear when targeting them in Lake Conjola — you will be pleasantly surprised.

BELOW: Not a bad morning's work on the shores of Lake Conjola.

23.7 THE STEPS

From late October to May there are usually plenty of poddy mullet about for bait. Either drift parallel to the steps or anchor on the edge of the drop off for dusky flathead and large bream. This is also another great spot to work soft plastics in deep water for those large dusky flathead. Jewfish can be caught here as well on the run-up tide.

23.8 WHITING ALLEY

As the name states this is a very good spot to target whiting on both the run-up and run-out tides. Tube, beach and blood worms are the go. You could also go and pump some pink nippers. Live poddy mullet will attract a few of the big dusky flathead. The best time of the year is from November to April.

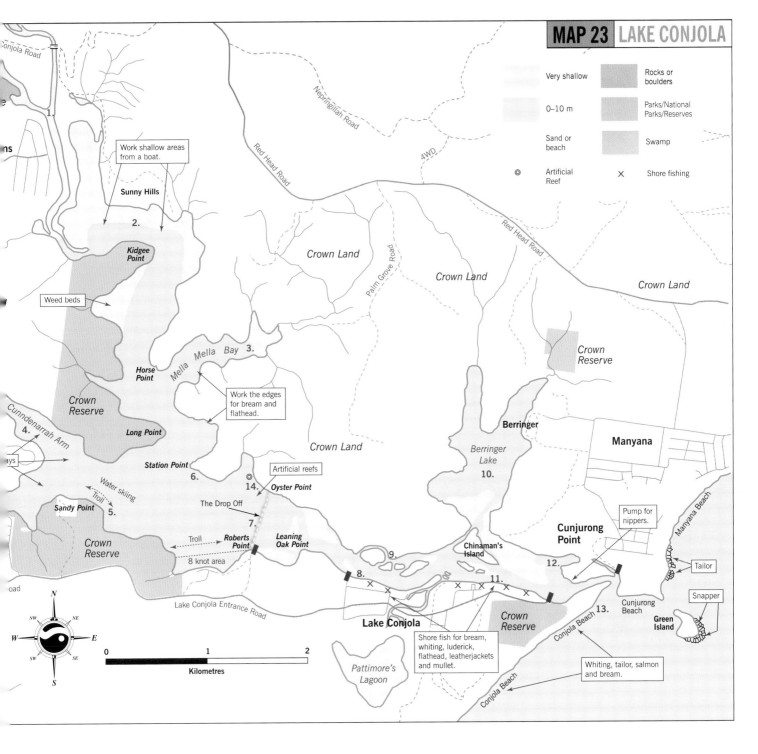

MAP 23 | LAKE CONJOLA

Legend:

Very shallow

0–10 m

Sand or beach

◎ Artificial Reef

Rocks or boulders

Parks/National Parks/Reserves

Swamp

× Shore fishing

Map labels:

Conjola Road

Nepringilah Road

Red Head Road

4WD

Work shallow areas from a boat.

Sunny Hills

Kidgee Point

Weed beds

Crown Land

Crown Land

Crown Land

Crown Reserve

Crown Reserve

Mella Mella Bay

Horse Point

Work the edges for bream and flathead.

Long Point

Cunndenarrah Arm

Crown Land

Berringer

Berringer Lake

Manyana

Manyana Beach

Station Point

Water skiing

Troll

Sandy Point

Crown Reserve

Artificial reefs

Oyster Point

The Drop Off

Troll

Roberts Point

8 knot area

Leaning Oak Point

Cunjurong Point

Pump for nippers.

Chinaman's Island

Tailor

Snapper

Lake Conjola Entrance Road

Lake Conjola

Shore fish for bream, whiting, luderick, flathead, leatherjackets and mullet.

Crown Reserve

Cunjurong Beach

Conjola Beach

Green Island

Whiting, tailor, salmon and bream.

Pattimore's Lagoon

Conjola Beach

N NW NE W E SW SE S

0   1   2
Kilometres

23.9   THE SHED

I have found this spot to fish best on the run-out tide for bream, blue swimmer crabs, whiting and luderick. Fish in close to the shore with long leaders and a size 2 bean or ball sinker that is above the swivel.

23.10   BERRINGER LAKE

This is very shallow water, but can be successfully fished with a small flat-bottomed boat, canoe or kayak. Best fish an hour either side of those very high, high tides for bream, whiting and dusky flathead with small surface poppers and lightly weighted soft plastics. Mullet and garfish can be berleyed up here as well.

23.11   CARAVAN PARK

Fish off the shore for bream, whiting, dusky flathead, small tailor, garfish and leatherjackets. The odd flounder has been caught here at the top of the tide. This is also a great stretch of shoreline to target luderick with green weed and a float.

23.12   THE FLATS

Pink nippers and squirt worms can be pumped here during the lower parts of the tides. With this bait you can either fish the flats at high tide or move to another spot in the lake. Bream, whiting and flathead are the main species caught. Troll or work soft plastics along the edge of the channel for dusky flathead on a run-out tide.

23.13   CONJOLA BEACH

Fish here for Australian salmon, tailor, bream, whiting, jewfish and dart. An angler once came up to me and asked what type of fish he had caught. It was a mullet and he had twelve of them in his bag. The biggest was about a kilo and the smallest was about 400 grams. All were caught on beach worms.

23.14 FISHERIES ARTIFICAL REEF

Corner 1	S 35 15 632	E150 28 313
Corner 2	S 35 15 628	E 150 28 330
Corner 3	S 35 15 668	E 150 28 320
Corner 4	S 35 15 664	E 150 28 344

The artificial reefs are being constructed using existing 'Reef Ball' technology. Reef balls are individual reef modules cast from a single mould. The Reef Ball modules are a patented mould supplied by the Reef Ball Development Group and are made from a special mix of concrete that enhances marine growth while withstanding saltwater corrosion.

The Department is using 'Mini-Bay Reef Balls', which when placed together on the bottom in varying numbers, form small artificial reefs of different sizes. The individual reef ball modules create habitat for marine fish, algae and crustaceans and can be deployed, moved or retrieved if necessary.

You can target yellowtail, mullet, snapper, whiting, dusky flathead, bream, flounder, crabs and jewfish at this artificial reef.

BOAT RAMPS SUSSEX INLET — ST GEORGES BASIN TO LAKE CONJOLA

Name	Make	Condition	No of Lanes	Wash Down	Lights	Fish Clean	BBQ	Toilets
Map 21　St Georges Basin								
Basin View Street St Georges Basin	Concrete	Good	2	Yes	Yes	Yes	Yes	Yes
Erowal Bay St George's Basin	Concrete	Poor	2	No	Yes	Yes	No	No
Island Point Road St Georges Basin	Concrete	Average	3	No	Yes	No	No	Yes
Sanctuary Point St Georges Basin	Concrete	Poor	1	Yes	Yes	No	Yes	Yes
Wrights Beach St Georges Basin	Concrete	Poor	1	No	No	No	No	No
Map 22　Sussex Inlet								
Boat Harbour Drive Sussex Inlet	Dirt	Poor	1	No	No	No	No	No
Sussex Rd Sussex Inlet	Concrete	Poor	1	No	No	No	No	No
Lakehaven Drive Sussex Inlet	Concrete	Good	4	Yes	Yes	Yes	Yes	Yes
Neilson Lane Sussex Inlet	Concrete	Average	1	Yes	Yes	Yes	Yes	Yes
Map 23　Lake Conjola								
Conjola Beach Lake Conjola	Concrete	Good	1	Yes	No	No	No	Yes
Fisherman's Paradise Rd Lake Conjola	Concrete	Good	1	Yes	No	Yes	No	Yes
Cunjurong Rd Lake Conjola	Concrete	Poor	1	No	No	No	Yes	Yes
Yooralla Bay Lake Conjola	Bitumen	Average	1	No	No	No	No	No

TACKLE SHOPS SUSSEX INLET — ST GEORGES BASIN TO LAKE CONJOLA

COASTAL ANGLER
2692 Princes Highway Wandandian
PHONE: (02) 9443 6091

DAGS FISHING TACKLE
Currently moving
PHONE: 0417 205552

OUTDOORS AND BEYOND
65 Owen Street Huskisson
PHONE: (02) 4441 6868

BAY AND BASIN MARINE
152 Island Point Road St Georges Basin
PHONE: (02) 4443 4361

SUSSEX TACKLE SHOP
168 Jacobs Drv Sussex Inlet
PHONE: (02) 4441 1660

LAKE CONJOLA LIQUOR STORE
4 Milhan Street Conjola
PHONE: (02) 4456 1828

CHAPTER 5
ULLADULLA
Mollymook to Bawley Point

Not everyone in your family may be into fishing, but who cares when you visit this stretch of coastline. There is something here for everyone, even if they don't fish. Ulladulla harbour is the focal point of the local fishing industry and you can sample the bounteous fare, fresh from the trawlers, at one of the award winning restaurants. In Ulladulla's CBD you will find supermarkets, real estate agents, shops, offices and banks as well as a wide variety of accommodation at the leading hotels, motels and guest houses.

Ulladulla hosts many festivals and events during the year. Try to visit in Easter when the Blessing of the Fleet Festival is held. This is a traditional ceremony which is held to pray for the safety of the fishing fleet and its crews during the fishing season. Another colourful and attractive festival is the Food & Wine Festival which is held annually.

The Burrill Lake, a beautiful coastal lake, is located 5km south of Ulladulla. The Princes Highway crosses the eastern arm of the lake only metres from the sea but its main expanse reaches inland almost to the town of Milton and cannot be seen from the highway. It is more than worth the effort to spend some time here and take a close look at the lake's attractions, for both its fishing potential as well as its beautiful surroundings.

Bawley Point is another one of those small beachside towns that is off the main highway so is mostly passed by. Next time you are down this way you should take the detour to the coast and have a look for yourself. You will be pleasantly surprised.

Kingfish can be caught while fishing off the rocks in the Ulladulla region, just like this one caught by Andrew McGovern.

MAP 24 ULLADULLA HARBOUR

Situated on its famous and picturesque harbour, Ulladulla is the commercial and retail centre for the Coastal Resort district. You can swim at a number of beaches at your doorstep or visit other magnificent beaches only a few minutes drive north or south.

Neighbouring towns Milton, Mollymook, Burrill Lake are all within five minutes drive. Jervis Bay Marine Park is 40 minutes north and Batemans Bay is 40 minutes south. You can take the kids for a fish off the western side of the harbour for bream and flathead on a rising tide.

24.1 MOLLYMOOK BEACH

Mollymook is the beachside paradise of the Coastal Resort area of the NSW south coast. Within easy distance of Canberra and Sydney, Mollymook is popular with many people as the ideal escape location any time of the year. Mollymook is located only minutes from the harbour port of Ulladulla and historic rural Milton. These three areas complement each other with their own special features and ambience.

The surrounding districts offer an abundance of nature's delights with spectacular scenery, forested mountains and myriad fascinating waterways. Mollymook is best known for its excellent surf beach of sweeping clean sands and clear waters and its neighbouring lush green golf course.

Excellent surf fishing, especially over summer when the water is warmer. Bream, salmon, tailor and the occasional small bronze whaler sharks can be caught in the morning. At night your best bet is the southern corner near the golf club where you can catch garfish and mullet. Best fishing with an incoming tide.

24.2 THE GOLF COURSE

If you have a boat you could try trolling skirted and deep diving lures around this section of the harbour for kingfish, tailor and the odd Australian salmon.

24.3 ULLADULLA HEAD

Fish the deep water that is found off this headland for tailor, snapper, bream and kingfish.

24.4 ULLADULLA HARBOUR

Ulladulla Harbour is situated in the Shoalhaven which is renowned for its white sandy beaches, great surfing and fishing, scenic rivers and lakes with national parks and mountain ranges as a backdrop.

24.5 THE PIER

Ideal access for all fisherman. Great location for the family with nearby takeaway stalls and toilets. For the kids a handline and some sort of food is all you need to try catch some of the smaller species of fish. For the more ardent fisherman fishing at dusk or night on a run up tide is your best bet to catch some trevally, leather jacket or tailor of legal size.

24.6 THE OCEAN POOL

Fish here is big seas for bream, drummer and silver trevally on a rising tide. Fish with a small ball sinker down onto the top of the bait.

24.7 NORTH FACE

If there has been a bit of a sea running from the south for a few days, the north face of the point is worth a shot for tailor, bream, squid, drummer and snapper. But be wary of the seas at high tide.

24.8 THE LIGHTHOUSE CHANNEL

Is situated at the end of Warden Headlands, below the lighthouse. Best fishing is during summer in the early morning where you can catch bream, blackfish and salmon. Fishing with an incoming tide is more productive because the rising water provides fish with new feeding grounds.

The Channel only fishes well when white water breaks over the outer reef. It is usually safe but plates are needed. In calm seas with an eastern swell, try along by deep hole on the north side. With a south eastern swell, try the south east corner and south side.

24.9 RENNIES BEACH

Rennies Beach fishes well after a big southerly blow. For bream use crab and pilchard fillets and fish very light. For salmon and tailor use pilchards with no sinker. There is usually plenty of cabbage available.

24.10 RACECOURSE BEACH

Racecourse Beach is located in the township of Ulladulla. The beach is approximately one kilometre long, with a small headland close to the centre. The beach is a popular surfing location, while swimming can be hazardous due to rocks and rips. Australian salmon, tailor, bream, whiting and jewfish can be targeted at this small, but very productive beach.

Carl Dubois just loves catching kingfish out of his Hobie Mirage kayak while using soft plastics.

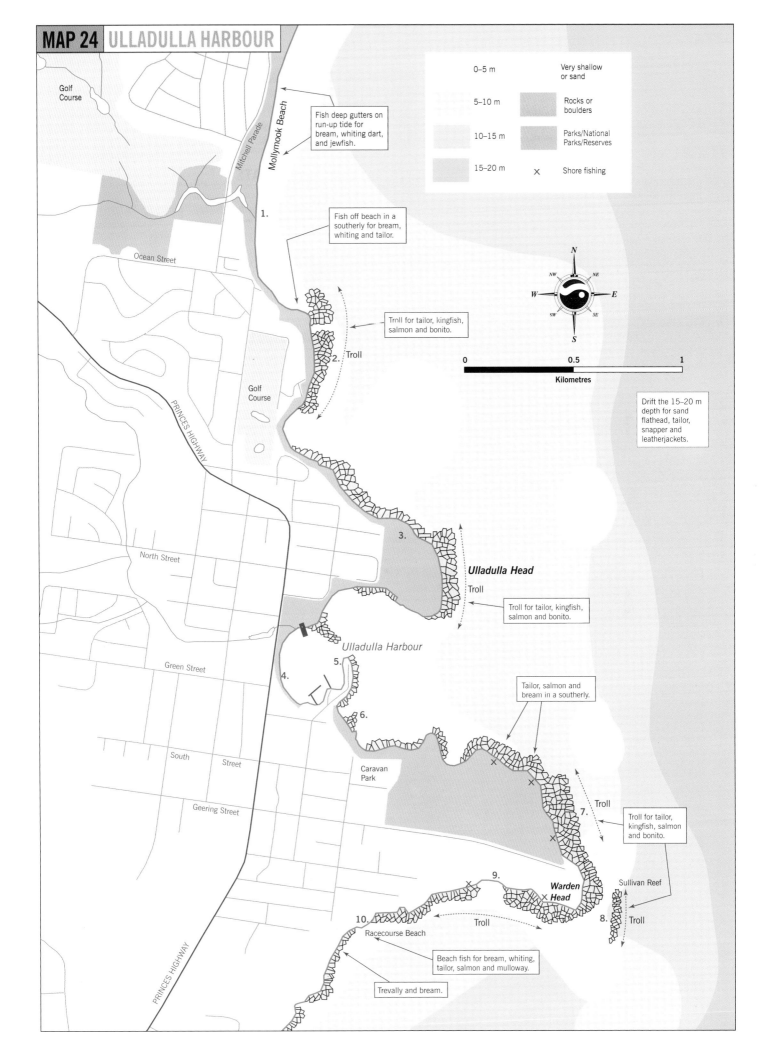

MAP 24 ULLADULLA HARBOUR

0–5 m — Very shallow or sand

5–10 m — Rocks or boulders

10–15 m

15–20 m — Parks/National Parks/Reserves

× — Shore fishing

Golf Course

Mollymook Beach

Mitchell Parade

Fish deep gutters on run-up tide for bream, whiting dart, and jewfish.

Ocean Street

1.

Fish off beach in a southerly for bream, whiting and tailor.

Golf Course

Troll for tailor, kingfish, salmon and bonito.

2. Troll

PRINCES HIGHWAY

0   0.5   1
Kilometres

Drift the 15–20 m depth for sand flathead, tailor, snapper and leatherjackets.

North Street

3.

Ulladulla Head

Troll

Troll for tailor, kingfish, salmon and bonito.

Green Street

Ulladulla Harbour

5.

4.

6.

Tailor, salmon and bream in a southerly.

South Street

Caravan Park

×

×

Geering Street

7. Troll

Troll for tailor, kingfish, salmon and bonito.

×

Sullivan Reef

9.

Warden Head ×

×

8. Troll

10.

Racecourse Beach

Troll

PRINCES HIGHWAY

Beach fish for bream, whiting, tailor, salmon and mulloway.

Trevally and bream.

MAP 25 BURRILL LAKE

This beautiful coastal lake is located five km south of Ulladulla. Most of its shores retain their natural bush land and forest cover and views west across the lake to Pigeon House Mountain create a beautiful natural setting. The Princes Highway crosses the eastern arm of the lake only metres from the sea but its main expanse reaches inland almost to the town of Milton and cannot be seen from the highway.

To see the upper parts of the lake you can visit Kings Point via its access road, west off the highway, north of the Burrill Lake township. At Kings Point, the lake is deep, quiet and tranquil. The local water ski club have their clubhouse, picnic area and launching ramp at Kings Point and there is water skiing here at weekends and during holiday periods.

Burrill Lake inlet and beaches are to the east of the highway. Take the road to Dolphin Point where there are some magnificent coastal views and picnic areas for a break. Burrill Lake offers boating, sailing, windsurfing, swimming and prawning (in season). Boats, canoes, skis and kayaks are available for hire.

25.1   THE BRIDGE

There have been times when I have travelled over this bridge and the anglers have been shoulder to shoulder fishing for luderick on the run-in and run-out tides. Now this is not always the case, as sometimes you can fish here and catch nothing. It pays to walk to the bridge with a small amount of berley and throw it in the water and see if anything comes up for it. Luderick, bream, whiting, mullet and dusky flathead can be caught from the shore on either

Work the steep shoreline of Burrill Lake with either lures, soft plastics and hard bodied lures for bream, snapper and flathead. Those of you that prefer to bait fish can anchor and berley for the same fish species.

side of the bridge. You could also anchor on either side of the bridge and berley while fishing the in-coming or out-going tide, that is if the entrance is open.

25.2   THE FLATS

This area is worth working surface lures, poppers and lightly weighted soft plastics for bream, whiting, luderick and dusky flathead.

25.3   LUDERICK RUN

Great stretch of shoreline for anchoring and float fishing for luderick. Bream and whiting can also be caught here beside the weed beds. Mullet and garfish will occasionally come up your berley trail. Not a bad place to catch a few blue swimmer crabs as well.

25.4   THE STEPS

It has been a while since I have fished the steps for dusky flathead. Start up in the weed beds on a run-in tide and slowly work you way out into the deeper water for dusky flathead with live poddy mullet and soft plastics. Chris and I managed to get 18 dusky flathead here in three hours.

25.5   BURRLI LAKE DRIVE

Try trolling this stretch of shoreline for dusky flathead, bream, tailor and the odd jewfish. You can also try putting out a few witches hats for a blue swimmer or two. I prefer to use mullet frames in the witches hats for the crabs. Squid can also be caught here when the water is fairly clear.

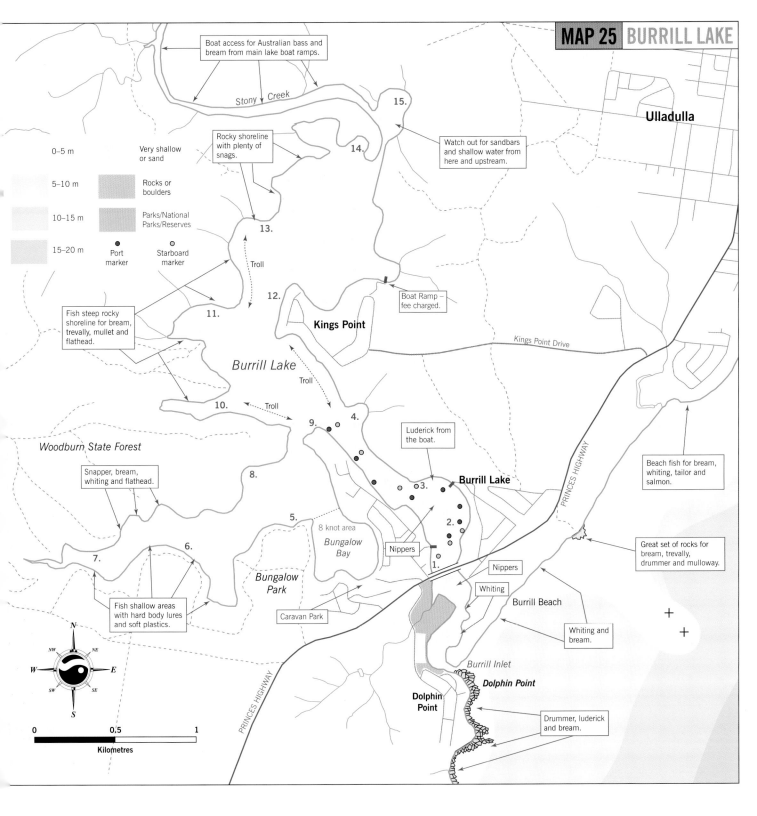

MAP 25 BURRILL LAKE

Boat access for Australian bass and bream from main lake boat ramps.

Stony Creek

Ulladulla

15.

14.

Rocky shoreline with plenty of snags.

Watch out for sandbars and shallow water from here and upstream.

0–5 m — Very shallow or sand

5–10 m — Rocks or boulders

10–15 m — Parks/National Parks/Reserves

15–20 m

• Port marker

○ Starboard marker

13.

Troll

Boat Ramp – fee charged.

12.

Kings Point

11.

Kings Point Drive

Fish steep rocky shoreline for bream, trevally, mullet and flathead.

Burrill Lake

Troll

10. Troll

9. 4.

Luderick from the boat.

Woodburn State Forest

8.

Burrill Lake

3.

Snapper, bream, whiting and flathead.

Beach fish for bream, whiting, tailor and salmon.

5.

8 knot area

Bungalow Bay

2.

Nippers

1.

PRINCES HIGHWAY

6.

Great set of rocks for bream, trevally, drummer and mulloway.

7.

Bungalow Park

Nippers

Whiting

Burrill Beach

Fish shallow areas with hard body lures and soft plastics.

Caravan Park

Whiting and bream.

N
NW NE
W E
SW SE
S

Burrill Inlet

Dolphin Point

PRINCES HIGHWAY

Dolphin Point

0   0.5   1

Kilometres

Drummer, luderick and bream.

25.6   LAKE ROAD

Try trolling here for tailor and dusky flathead. Anchor and berley where the water gets a bit deeper for bream, flathead, flounder, crabs and dusky flathead.

25.7   SNAPPER REACH

I stumbled across this spot while chasing dusky flathead in a competition a few years back. My mate and I managed to catch five legal snapper here in a short period. All were caught on striped tuna and very little lead for weight. Hey, but don't forget to target bream and flathead here on the rising tide. The snapper were caught on a falling tide and in the earlier part of the morning.

25.8   FLATHEAD RUN

As the names suggest this stretch of shoreline will at times produce a lot of dusky flathead in the shallow at high tide and in the deeper water towards the bottom of the tide. There is not a lot of water movement up in this part of the lake, so you will need to apply the berley and fish as light as possible. Also try putting out a few witches hats while you are up there. Blue swimmer crabs are great when they are cooked on the barbeque in sweet chili sauce.

25.9   WILLY'S HOLE

Many years ago I fished Burrill Lakes for a week straight and every time I motored up through the channel and out into the main part of

of tailor. Try trolling here on quieter days of the week or on overcast and rainy days.

25.13   SNAG CITY

The last time I fished here I spent a fair amount of time fishing as many snags as I could find. There were snags on the shoreline, just under the water level and down in the deeper water. Bream, snapper, silver trevally and Australian bass can be targeted in these snags.

25.14   MUDDY POINT

All of the flathead that I have caught here over the years of fishing this stretch of water, have been very dark on top and a very creamy colour on the under belly side.

25.15   STONEY CREEK

This small and narrow creek winds its way up to the back of Milton. Bream, flathead, whiting, mullet, garfish, jewfish and Australian bass can be caught here. You will need to take care when fishing as there are a number of sand bars, sunken trees and boulders throughout the creek. I ran up onto a shallow sand bar while fishing with my son. Boy, did we come to a sudden stop.

the lake I passed a small clinker boat that was named Willy's Boat. It got the better of me, so one the fourth day I pulled up beside this boat to find an all-female crew sitting under the canopy. They were targeting bream, whiting and flathead on the run-up tide. They were sisters from Ulladulla and the boat belonged to their brother who had just passed away the week before. They promised Willy they would take the boat out for a fish when he had gone. At the time the ladies were in their eighties and that was ten years ago. I still wonder if they are alive and are still fishing. You also catch silver trevally, snapper and jewfish here on the run-up tide.

25.10   SHADOWS
COVE

Shadows Cove has very steep banks which are dotted with a number of rock bars and snags along its foreshores. These areas are great for casting lures, soft plastics and baits for bream, dusky flathead, silver trevally and the odd jewfish.

25.11   TENNIS COURT

This rocky shoreline will hold bream and dusky flathead throughout most of the tide. Just work your way out to the deeper water as the tide drops.

25.12   KINGS POINT

When there are no water skiers around this point can hold schools

RIGHT: Check out the size of this Burrill Lake yellowfin bream that Carl caught.

MAP 26 WARDEN HEAD AT ULLADULLA TO NORTH HEAD AT BATEMANS BAY BEACHES AND ROCKS

26.1 BURRILL BEACH

What a great little beach this is. There is easy access to the beach and the quality of the whiting and bream you can catch here is great. I prefer to use a paternoster rig when fishing from the beach, as it gives me two baited hooks. I can have a pipi on one and a piece of beach worm on the other. You could also try using a half pilly on one hook and a strip of mullet on the other for bream and flathead. If I am targeting jewfish from this beach I will use a running sinker down onto a swivel and about a metre of leader.

26.2 WAIRO BEACH

Wairo Beach is situated between Burrill Lake and Tabourie Lake. Enjoy a bush walk in nearby Meroo National Park, or fish, swim, canoe or just relax with a picnic on the beach.

26.3 LAKE TABOURIE

Situated on the coastline, only 10 minutes south of Ulladulla is the thriving beach village of Tabourie Lake. The tiny township is every fisherman's dream with the abundance of aquatic life and the fantastic water sports facilities. Tabourie Lake has something for everybody. Go fishing, hire a canoe or go water skiing on the lake. If water sports are not your thing, the beautiful national parks surrounding the lake provide great walking tracks, picnics and mountain climbing.

At low tide you can walk across to Crampton Island and explore. The island offers rock shelves, and coastal heath – nature at its best. There are excellent views back to Pidgeon House Mountain which is 15 minutes drive from Lake Tabourie and part of the magnificent Budawang National park. The half day bushwalk up Pidgeon House is recommended.

26.4 TERMEIL BEACH

If you like chasing jewfish, sharks and rays you could try targeting them after dark off this beach. There are usually a number of deep holes and gutters found on this beach. During the day you could target bream and whiting, and in the morning and late afternoons you could cast out a whole pilchard or garfish on a set of ganged hooks for tailor and Australian salmon.

26.5 MEROO POINT

This is one of those points that slide off into the water and is surrounded by sand. You can walk to Meroo Point by starting at the southern end of the beach south of Nuggan Head. Once you climb up and over Nuggan Head you will come to another smaller beach on the northern side of Nuggen.

Eastern wirrahs may be a pest when fishing off the rocks for other species, but there are some anglers out there who like to eat them. They are commonly known as boot.

Cross this small beach and you are at the southern end of the point.

Once here you can fish for snapper, drummer, luderick, tailor, Australian salmon, flathead, dart and silver trevally. You will also find great gutters on either end of this small, but very productive headland.

26.6 MEROO LAKE BEACH

This small moon shaped beach fishes well for Australian salmon, tailor, bream and whiting. The beach really fires for all of the above fish species and jewfish when Meroo Lake has busted out and is emptying into the sea. Try using live prawns and mullet when this happens.

26.7 NUGGAN POINT

When the seas are up the northern side of Nuggan Point is a great place to fish into deep water for drummer, bream, silver trevally, tailor and Australian salmon. When the seas calm down a bit you can target snapper, squid and luderick out towards the front of the point on the north-eastern side.

If there is a bit of a swell and wind coming from a northerly direction the small platform in the corner on the southern side is worth a fish for bream, silver trevally, Australian salmon, tailor, drummer and luderick. You will be fishing into a small cove that has a mixture of broken rocks, sand and weed.

26.8 MURRAMARANG BEACH

Murramarang Beach is one of three beaches located in the small coastal village of Bawley Point and is approximately 2.5 kilometres south of Ulladulla. Parking here is not a problem as you virtually park within ten metres of the beach. Fishing at the northern end of the beach is best done when the winds are coming in from the north-west to northerly direction. If you walk about a kilometre south you will come to a set of rocks and a deep gutter that you can fish for bream, whiting, Australian salmon and tailor. Whole pilchards and

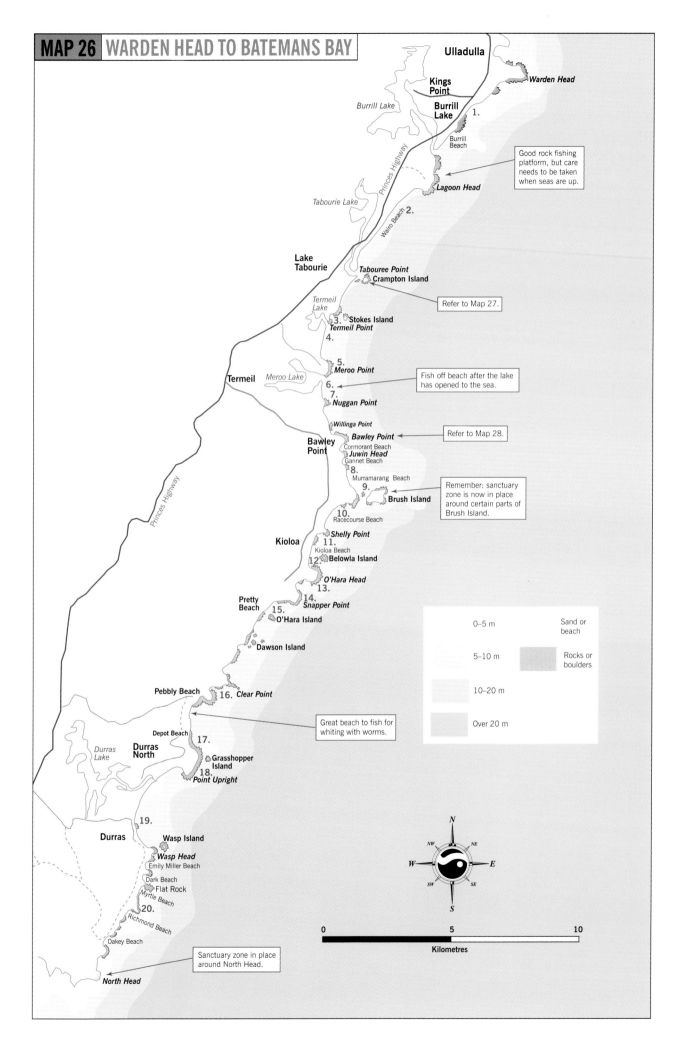

MAP 26 WARDEN HEAD TO BATEMANS BAY

Ulladulla

Kings
Point

Warden Head

Burrill Lake

Burrill
Lake

1.

Burrill
Beach

Good rock fishing
platform, but care
needs to be taken
when seas are up.

Lagoon Head

Tabourie Lake

2.

Wairo Beach

Lake
Tabourie

Tabouree Point
Crampton Island

Refer to Map 27.

*Termeil
Lake*

3. Stokes Island
Termeil Point

4.

5.
Meroo Point

Termeil

Meroo Lake

6.

Fish off beach after the lake
has opened to the sea.

7.
Nuggan Point

Willinga Point

Bawley Point

Refer to Map 28.

Bawley
Point

Cormorant Beach
Juwin Head
Gannet Beach
8.
Murramarang Beach

9.
Brush Island

Remember: sanctuary
zone is now in place
around certain parts of
Brush Island.

10.
Racecourse Beach

Shelly Point

Kioloa

11.
Kioloa Beach
12. Belowla Island

O'Hara Head
13.

14.
Snapper Point

Pretty
Beach

15.
O'Hara Island

Dawson Island

Pebbly Beach

16. *Clear Point*

Great beach to fish for
whiting with worms.

Depot Beach

17.

Durras
North

*Durras
Lake*

Grasshopper
Island
18.
Point Upright

19.

Durras

Wasp Island

Wasp Head
Emily Miller Beach

Dark Beach
Flat Rock
Myrtle Beach

20.
Richmond Beach

Oakey Beach

Sanctuary zone in place
around North Head.

North Head

Princes Highway

0–5 m	Sand or beach
5–10 m	Rocks or boulders
10–20 m	
Over 20 m	

N
NW NE
W   E
SW SE
S

0   5   10
Kilometres

garfish on a set of ganged hooks, ball sinker down onto the bait for bream and pink nippers, pipis, beach or blood worms for the whiting.

26.9   INSIDE BRUSH ISLAND

This small point can produce some of the best Australian salmon and tailor fishing on the south coast. Especially when there has been a bit of a sea running from the south and the wind is offshore. Fish in and around the boulders and washes that are found here for bream, drummer and silver trevally.

26.10   RACECOURSE BEACH

Racecourse Beach is a broad, sandy beach that has a headland at both ends. While fishing at the northern end you will see Brush Island. This is a nature reserve where landing is prohibited, but is a popular boat fishing spot. I have found that this beach can be great or bloody terrible. It all depends on the types of gutters that are there. They need to be deep, with a sand bar out the back and in the shape of a horse shoe to produce bream, Australian salmon, tailor and whiting. Best baits are whole pilchards, pink nipper and beach and blood worms.

26.11   SHELLY POINT

If you are staying at the caravan park at Racecourse Beach at Bawley Point it is a 20 minute walk south to this very productive point. Drummer, luderick, bream, silver trevally, groper, tailor and Australian salmon can be caught here. I have found the two to three hours of the rising tide and two hours of the failing tide to give the best results. Berley is essential here for success.

The northern side is a set of small gutters and large boulders with patches of sand in between. As you walk south the water tends to deepen, but the fishing is not as good as the middle and northern end of the point.

Andrew McGovern caught this great snapper while fishing off the rocks.

26.12   KIOLOA BEACH

The beach here fishes reasonably well for bream, whiting, flathead and tailor and the odd jewfish at night. There is a small sandy boat ramp that is not great, but can give you access to some great offshore fishing. You will need to make sure that your boat is sea worthy. I have fished Kioloa a few times and there are a couple of good land based spots as well.

Offshore fishing you could try drifting for flathead north of Kioloa Island and north of Bawley point. Snapper, morwong, tailor, leatherjackets and other reef fish are on offer. There is a big bombie off Kioloa and several off Brush Island, so be careful. When the fishing is not that great you can have good fun feeding the big rays around the ramp when cleaning your catch.

26.13   O'HARA HEAD

At times the fishing from O'Hara Head can be excellent. Try here for drummer, snapper, tuna, kingfish, tailor, bream, silver trevally, luderick and groper.

26.14   SNAPPER POINT

Snapper Point is just south of Merry Beach and is easily reached from a track at the back of the camping ground at Pretty Beach. It is one of the few deep water fishing locations on this part of the coast.

The game season at Snapper Point runs until late April, depending on the prevailing currents.

Pike, squid, garfish and yellowtail can be caught from the point. These are used as live baits for kingfish, mack and yellowfin tuna and bonito. You can also target snapper, drummer, luderick, silver trevally and bream from either side of the point.

26.15   O'HARA ISLAND

If you have a boat this small island is great for chasing, tailor, salmon, snapper and bream in the washes. You could also try trolling a few lures for kingfish, bonito and tuna around the front of the island, but be careful on the shallow rocks and reefs that are found here.

26.16   PEBBLY BEACH

Pebbly beach can be a great to head too on those days when there is a bit of south swell with northerlies blowing. You can expect to find some well formed gutters here. This spot is famous for its kangaroos that just hang around the beach front. It's quite a surreal feeling strolling down to the water's edge for a surf with kangaroos bounding all over the place. Pebbly beach is definitely something to experience. Produces whiting and bream in the summer months, while tailor and Australian salmon are the go on either whole garfish or WA pilchards.

Chris was very glad he had his wet weather gear and rock cleats on. He definitely looks a bit wet here.

along to Point Upright are excellent for snapper, luderick, drummer, groper and bream. These rocks are exposed to the elements, so care needs to be taken when fishing them.

26.18   POINT UPRIGHT

Great place to target bream, drummer, luderick, silver trevally and groper in one of the many washes that are found here. You can also try casting out wide for snapper and jewfish on a rising tide. Half fillets of mullet, yellowtail, bonito and tuna strips are the go. Also try using squid or octopus that can be caught on this rock ledge.

26.19   DURRAS LAKE

The fishing along the entire length of this beach can be excellent at times. Target Australian salmon, tailor, bream, whiting and flathead on a rising tide. I find that if I restrict myself to carrying one rod and a hungry bag I can become very mobile. If I am fishing a gutter and there is not much happening on this beach I can quickly move to the next gutter and not have too much to take with me. Just a small tackle box with the essentials, some bait, a knife and a bag to put the fish in.

26.17   DEPOT BEACH

Depot beach has a tendency to produce some great beach breaks when the sand is right. The banks here are pretty consistent and are protected from being torn up by the big southerly busters. This spot can produce some great fishing for whiting and bream. There's plenty of empty beach and reef breaks to be found around this area for the keen angler. I have also found that the rocks that are running

26.20   DURRAS SOUTH

South of Durras you can try fishing for snapper and bream at Wasp Head, luderick at Flat Rock Island, drummer, bream and luderick on the point just south of Myrtle Beach. The rocks at Oaky Beach are worth a shot for bream, drummer, snapper and luderick on a rising tide and North Head is always good for drummer, groper and snapper.

MAP 27 CRAMPTON ISLAND – LAKE TABOURIE

You can fish in the lake, beach or off the rocks at Crampton island. Surf at either the north or south beach, it does not matter which way the swell is coming from, the surf is always up. The lake is fantastic for canoeing and kayaking and there is no better way to fish.

27.1   SAND SPIT — NORTH

This stretch of sand spit can usually be crossed at half tide to gain access to the fishing on Crampton Island. I find that you will need to coincide your outing to about three hours either side of the high tide. If you can't cross due to the depth of the water on the spit you can always fish from the mainland side with pipis, pink nippers, beach and blood worms for bream, flathead and whiting

27.2   THE BOULDERS

This area is reasonably shallow at the best of times. Try fishing the rising tide and about one hour of the falling tide. Fish as light as possible for bream, drummer and luderick. I find that if I use half pillies, strips of mullet and tuna and bread for bait I seem to get the best results. Berley is a must.

27.3   SHALLOW REEF

Now, if you are after a bream or two this would have to be one of the island's better spots. Berley and fish as light as possible to get amongst the bream and drummer that come in here to feed on the rising and falling tides. Berley to get the best results.

If you are after a few Australian salmon, try using a whole pilchard on a set of ganged hooks while fishing off Crampton Island.

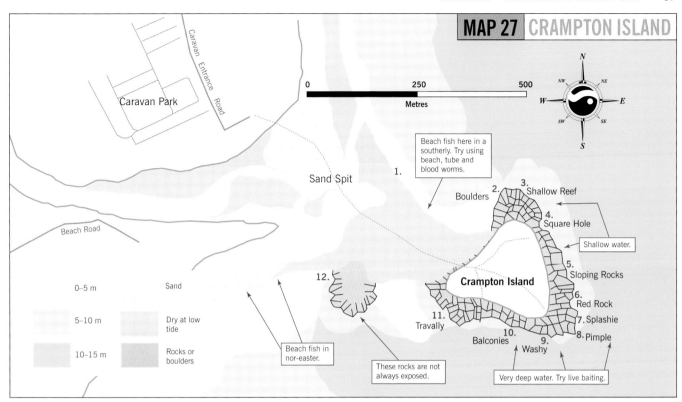

MAP 27 CRAMPTON ISLAND

Map labels:
- Caravan Park
- Caravan Entrance Road
- Sand Spit
- Beach Road
- 0 250 500 Metres
- 1. Beach fish here in a southerly. Try using beach, tube and blood worms.
- Boulders
- 2.
- 3. Shallow Reef
- 4. Square Hole
- Shallow water.
- Crampton Island
- 5. Sloping Rocks
- 6. Red Rock
- 7. Splashie
- 8. Pimple
- 9. Washy
- 10. Balconies
- 11. Travally
- 12.
- Very deep water. Try live baiting.
- Beach fish in nor-easter.
- These rocks are not always exposed.
- 0–5 m / Sand
- 5–10 m / Dry at low tide
- 10–15 m / Rocks or boulders

27.4 SQUARE HOLE

This place is only fishable when the seas are fair to calm. Berleying is an essential item when fishing here for bream, drummer, snapper and tailor on a falling tide.

27.5 SLOPPING ROCKS

Care needs to be taken when fishing here as the rocks do slope and they can be very slippery at times. Make sure that you are wearing the correct footwear or you may go for an unsuspected swim.

27.6 RED ROCK

Vey similar to the Square Hole. This place is only fishable when the seas are fair to calm. Berleying is an essential item when fishing here for bream, drummer, snapper and tailor on a falling tide.

27.7 SPLASHIE

A very wet spot to fish, so you will need to wear that wet weather gear. Good for bream, silver trevally, drummer and the odd luderick or two.

27.8 PIMPLE

When the seas are fair to calm you can fish here for drummer, bream, silver trevally and snapper on the rising tide.

27.9 WASHY

There are a number of small washes located here that will hold silver trevally, bream, drummer and luderick. Berley is essential to your success when fishing here.

27.10 THE BALCONIES

This is a deep water spot where you can cast whole pilchards or garfish on a set of ganged hooks for tailor, tuna, kingfish and

Cast out wide with a paternoster rig for snapper while fishing off Crampton Island. They can also be caught in the washes.

Australian salmon. You could also try spinning with a few different sizes of metal spinners. Also a great place to fish for drummer, bream and luderick. Fishing is safe up to a moderate sea.

27.11 TREVALLY

Fish here for bream, luderick, drummer, tailor, Australian salmon, snapper, jewfish and tuna. There has also been a few kingfish caught here when there has been a bit of a blow from the north.

27.12 SAND SPIT — SOUTH

You will need to coincide your outing to about three hours either side of the high tide. If you can't cross due to the depth of the water on the spit you can always fish from the mainland side with pipis, pink nippers, beach and blood worms for bream, flathead and whiting. Much the same as when you are fishing from the northern side of the spit.

MAP 28 BAWLEY POINT

Looking north to Brush Island from Racecourse Beach Caravan Park.

Bawley Point is a small township that is about six kilometres from the highway at a place called Termeil. There is plenty on offer here for the rock and beach angler. You could fish Bawley Point, Nuggen to the north of Bawley and Stinky to the south or Racecourse beach. There are a number of bed and breakfasts located here, as well as a caravan park, take away shops and a tackle shop.

28.1   BAWLEY BEACH NO 1.

I have found this beach to work the best after there has been a bit of a sea running. Good place to get a few beach worms. Fish for bream, whiting, silver trevally, tailor and Australian salmon.

28.2   BOAT RAMP

If you have a small and sea worthy boat you can launch from here when the seas are calm and fish for snapper, bream, drummer, tailor, Australian salmon and jewfish in one of the many washes found around this stretch of coast line.

28.3   THE GANTRY

When fishing from the gantry I have caught Australian salmon, tailor, silver trevally, bream, whiting and luderick. Not a good spot when the seas are very calm. There needs to be a bit of swell coming in to give the fish a bit of cover. Plenty of stingrays feed around the bottom of the Gantry. Best fished during those low light periods, overcast days and at night. Fishing on either side of the Gantry is also very good at times.

28.4   GARY'S SWIMMING HOLE

I have called this spot Gary's Swimming Hole as this is where I was fishing for silver trevally and bream on a falling tide with a few mates. I did see the small wave coming, but it managed to rip off my rock sandal, which caused me to fall over. The other guys I was fishing with at the time could only see half of my rod. This spot is a good spot to fish, but no matter how experienced you are, you don't know when the next wave may sneak up on you.

28.5   BREAM ROCKS

There are plenty of crevices and boulders in this part of the bay. Try fishing here when there is a bit of wash coming into the bay. Fish as light as possible or with a bobby cork or float. Very snaggy area.

A variety of flathead can be caught while fishing off the rocks. Look out for those sandy patches.

28.6   LUDERICK POINT

I have been fishing here with Alan and Vicky

MAP 28 BAWLEY POINT

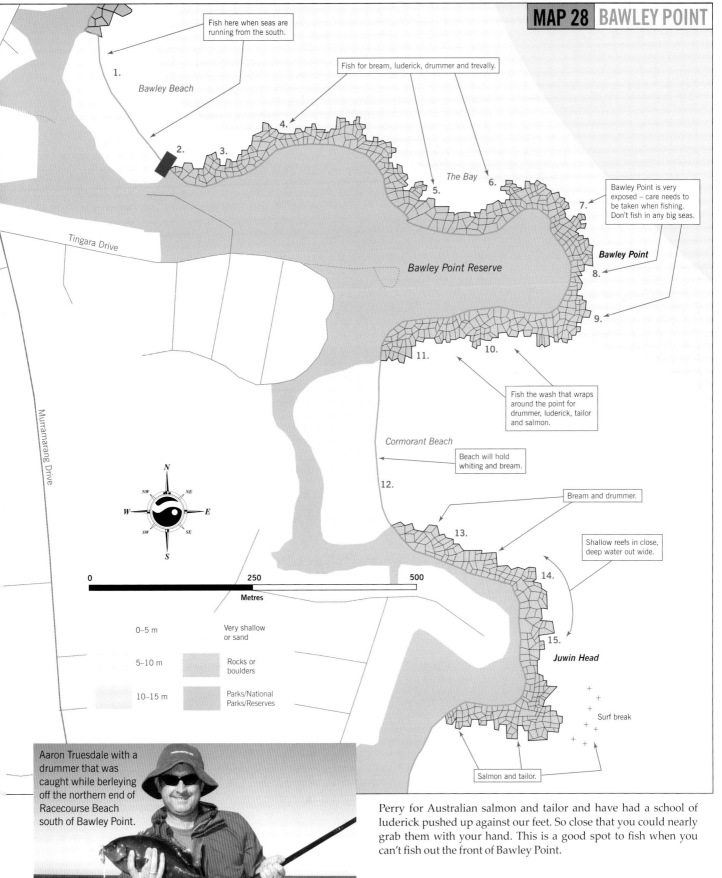

Fish here when seas are running from the south.

1.

Bawley Beach

2.

3.

4.

Fish for bream, luderick, drummer and trevally.

5.

6.

The Bay

7.

Bawley Point is very exposed – care needs to be taken when fishing. Don't fish in any big seas.

Bawley Point

8.

Bawley Point Reserve

9.

Tingara Drive

10.

11.

Fish the wash that wraps around the point for drummer, luderick, tailor and salmon.

Cormorant Beach

Beach will hold whiting and bream.

12.

Murramarang Drive

Bream and drummer.

13.

Shallow reefs in close, deep water out wide.

14.

15.

Juwin Head

N

NW *NE*

W *E*

SW *SE*

S

+ +

+

+ +

Surf break

+

0   250   500

Metres

+ +

0–5 m   Very shallow or sand

5–10 m   Rocks or boulders

10–15 m   Parks/National Parks/Reserves

Salmon and tailor.

Aaron Truesdale with a drummer that was caught while berleying off the northern end of Racecourse Beach south of Bawley Point.

Perry for Australian salmon and tailor and have had a school of luderick pushed up against our feet. So close that you could nearly grab them with your hand. This is a good spot to fish when you can't fish out the front of Bawley Point.

28.7   THE DROP AWAY

To successfully fish here you will either need to make a good cast of 50 to 60 metres with a paternoster rig or fish as light as possible and let your bait float around in the wash. This may mean that you will have to walk the bait around the corner with the wash. Bream, silver trevally, Australian salmon, tailor and snapper can be caught here. You will need to keep an eye on the waves at all times as they will wrap around the side of the point. Cunje, cabbage and crabs can be gathered for bait from here.

28.8   THE FRONT OF BAWLEY

The front of Bawley Point is not a place to be when there is any type of sea running as it is very flat and a wave can come up at you from the side. I have found that after there has been a sea of sorts and it has calmed down to just small waves hitting the rocks the bream will turn on the bite, especially if you use plenty of bread and pilchards for berley. Concentrate your fishing time to about an hour and a half each side of the top of the tide. Use as little lead as possible. Direct your cast towards the edge of the white water and keep your bait coming slowly back towards you. This will help prevent those unwanted snags.

28.9   THE WASHES

Try for luderick, tailor and Australian salmon, but remember to watch the seas as it does break here a fair bit.

28.10   SOUTH BAWLEY WASH

Good place to target luderick and bream in calm seas. You will need to use plenty of berley to get the fish on the chew.

28.11   THE CORNER

When the seas are up and you are struggling to find a spot to fish you could try here for bream, luderick, drummer, tailor and the odd jewfish and Australian salmon. Fish the top of the tide and down to about half-way for the best results.

28.12   BAWLEY BEACH NO 2

I have found this beach works the best after there has been a bit of a sea running. Good place to get a few beach worms. Fish for bream, whiting, silver trevally, tailor and Australian salmon. Either fish in the deep gutter that can form or fish adjacent to the rocks and beach.

28.13   ALLAN'S HOLE

Great place to chase luderick, drummer and bream on either side of the top of the tide. Fish as light as possible as there are plenty of snags, boulders and kelp to get caught in.

28.14   JUWIN HEAD LEDGE

When the sea are calm, fish here out wide for snapper, silver trevally, tailor and Australian salmon a couple of hours before the sun sets.

28.15   JUWIN BOMBIE

Close in there is some pretty rough reef, but if you can manage a cast of 25 to 30 metres you will get your bait into some prime fishing washes. Best baits are peeled prawns, mullet strips, cunje, tuna strips, pilchards and garfish. You will need to fish as light as possible and concentrate your efforts to about two hours either side of the top of the tide. Early morning and late afternoons would be the best time to fish here, unless you have an overcast day.

MAP 29 WRECK BAY TO DURRAS LAKE
— OFFSHORE GPS POINTS

29.1   CUDMIRRAH REEF
S 35 12 620   E 150 34 768

10 to 13 fathoms. Reef, boulders and broken shale bottom. Snapper, leatherjackets, sweep, morwong, pig fish and nannygai.

29.2   THE WIDE GROUND
S 35 14 057   E 150 35 292

16 fathoms. Drift this area for sand and tiger flathead. Snapper and tailor have been caught here as well.

29.3   THE OUTER REEF
S 35 15 388   E 150 36 998

The depth varies from 24 to 35 fathoms. Drift or anchor here for snapper, leatherjackets, sweep, morwong, pig fish and nannygai.

29.4   BROOKES DEEP REEF
S 35 15 810   E 150 36 180

60 metres. Fish here for bream, tarwhine, Australian salmon on the surface and snapper, leatherjackets, sweep, morwong, pig fish and nannygai. You can also try drifting for sand flathead on the edges of the reef.

29.5   REDHEAD REEF
S 35 15 049   E 150 33 065

15 to 20 fathoms for reddies, blue morwong, leatherjackets and pig fish. You can also try trolling this area as well for tuna, bonito and tailor on the surface.

29.6   MANYANNA BOMMIE
S 35 16 275   E 150 32 211

This bommie is very dangerous and it doesn't take much for it to break. Fish inside the bommie to Green Island for snapper, leatherjackets, sweep, morwong, bream and tarwhine.

29.7   BANNISTER PEAK
S 35 19 066   E 150 31 149

22 fathoms that comes up to 18 fathoms. Best fished from the top of the tide and down for kingfish and snapper from November to late January. Leatherjackets, sweep, morwong, pig fish and nannygai.

Try trolling with Tropic Angler skirted lures wide of Ulladulla.

MAP 29 WRECK BAY TO DURRAS LAKE — OFFSHORE GPS POINTS

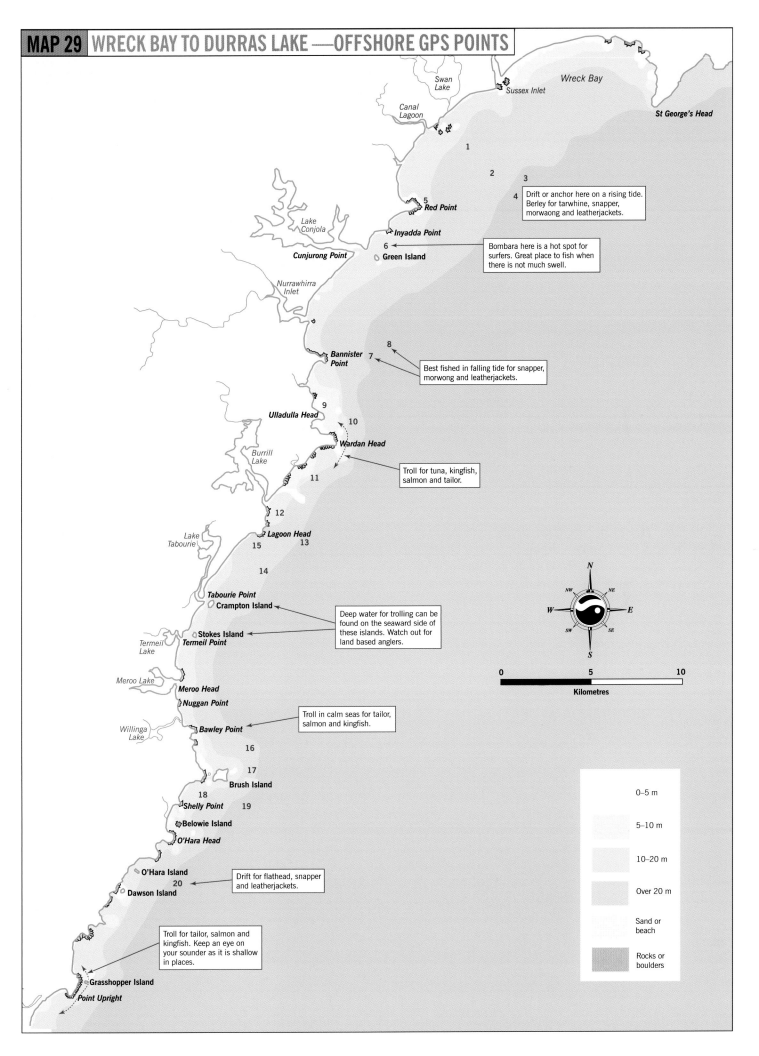

Swan Lake

Canal Lagoon

Wreck Bay

Sussex Inlet

St George's Head

1

2

3

4

Drift or anchor here on a rising tide. Berley for tarwhine, snapper, morwaong and leatherjackets.

5
Red Point

Inyadda Point

Lake Conjola

Cunjurong Point

6

Green Island

Bombara here is a hot spot for surfers. Great place to fish when there is not much swell.

Nurrawhirra Inlet

8

Bannister Point

7

Best fished in falling tide for snapper, morwong and leatherjackets.

9

Ulladulla Head

10

Burrill Lake

Wardan Head

Troll for tuna, kingfish, salmon and tailor.

11

12

Lake Tabourie

Lagoon Head

15

13

14

Tabourie Point

Crampton Island

Deep water for trolling can be found on the seaward side of these islands. Watch out for land based anglers.

Stokes Island
Termeil Point

Termeil Lake

Meroo Lake

Meroo Head

Nuggan Point

Willinga Lake

Bawley Point

Troll in calm seas for tailor, salmon and kingfish.

16

17

Brush Island

18

19

Shelly Point

Belowie Island

O'Hara Head

O'Hara Island

20

Dawson Island

Drift for flathead, snapper and leatherjackets.

Troll for tailor, salmon and kingfish. Keep an eye on your sounder as it is shallow in places.

Grasshopper Island

Point Upright

N
NW NE
W E
SW SE
S

0   5   10
Kilometres

0–5 m

5–10 m

10–20 m

Over 20 m

Sand or beach

Rocks or boulders

29.8 BANNISTER POINT EAST
S 35 19 066
E 150 32 217

All hard ground to the 65 metre mark. Fish for snapper, morwong, sweep, kingfish and mauri wrasse on this area and around the edges for sand and tiger flathead.

29.9 THE GOLF CLUB
S 35 20 272
E 150 29 091

One nautical mile east of the coast in about 10 fathoms of water. Good in a south-westerly wind for bream, tarwhine, leatherjackets, snapper and the odd morwong.

29.10 KINGFISH GROUND
S 35 22 084
E 150 32 174

Three nautical miles from Ulladulla Harbour. The inside edge of this reef comes up to 32 fathoms from about 40 fathoms. Fish on this drop-off for kingfish, snapper, bonito and the odd tuna.

There is nothing better than seeing a young angler getting a workout by a hard pulling kingfish.

29.11 BURRILL ROCKS WIDE
S 35 22 377   E 150 29 229

Look for the telephone line off Manyanna and under the rocks near the lighthouse. 80 fathoms. Snapper, morwong and leatherjackets.

29.12 BURRILL CLOSE
S 35 24 000   E 150 28 000

When the skies are clear try putting Pigeon House mountain over the Caravan Park for snapper, leatherjackets, sweep, morwong, pigfish and nannygai.

29.13 BIG WAIROA WIDE
S 35 25 212   E 150 28 211

Very hard reef found here in 36 fathoms. Try fishing for snapper, leatherjackets, sweep, morwong, pigfish and nannygai.

29.14 HARD REEF
S 35 26 800   E 150 26 500

This is another place that has a very hard reef found here in 20 fathoms. Fish for snapper, leatherjackets, sweep, morwong, pigfish and nannygai. Try drifting the edges for sand and tiger flathead.

29.15 TABOURIE BEACH
S 35 25 475   E 150 25 208

Two thirds of the way down the beach and up to 0.5 kilometres from the headland you can drift for snapper, groper, bream and morwong.

29.16 BRUSH ISLAND BOMBIE
S 35 32 000   E 150 25 700

3 nautical miles north-east of Kioloa. 9 fathoms deep on the inside and 18 fathoms on the outside. Fish for bream, snapper, morwong and leatherjackets.

29.17 BRUSH ISLAND ROCK SHELF
S 35 32 000   E 150 25 400

2.5 nautical miles north-east of Kioloa in 10 fathoms of water for morwong, snapper and silver trevally. Sand flathead can be caught around the edges of the rock shelf.

29.18 BRUSH ISLAND FLATHEAD DRIFT
S 35 22 400   E 150 24 900

Try drifting for sand and tiger flathead from the 9 fathoms mark to the 19 fathoms mark.

29.19 SAND FLATS AND GRAVEL
S 35 33 800   E 150 25 100

2 nautical miles east of Kioloa. Drift or anchor for snapper, leatherjackets, sweep, morwong, pigfish and nannygai.

29.20 DAWSON ISLANDS
S 35 35 300   E 150 21 700

Fish in close, about one kilometre from the islands in the east-south-east and up to 2 nautical miles out from the shore for snapper, leatherjackets, sweep, morwong, pigfish and nannygai.

BOAT RAMPS ULLADULLA — MOLLYMOOK TO BAWLEY POINT

Name	Make	Condition	No of Lanes	Wash Down	Lights	Fish Clean	BBQ	Toilets
Map 24 Ulladulla and Surrounds								
North Harbour Ulladulla	Concrete	Average	3	Yes	Yes	Yes	Yes	Yes
South Harbour Ulladulla	Concrete	Average	3	Yes	Yes	No	No	Yes
Narrawallee	Concrete	Average	1	No	Yes	Yes	No	Yes
Map 25 Burrill Lake								
Bungalow Bay Burrill Lake	Earth	Average	1	No	No	No	No	No
Kings Point Water Ski Club Burrill Lake	Concrete	Average	2	Yes	No	No	No	Yes
Maria Ave Burrill Lake	Concrete	Average	2	No	No	Yes	No	No
Northern Burrill Lake	Concrete	Average	1	No	Yes	No	No	No
Map 27 Crampton Island – Lake Tabourie								
Tabourie Lake	Concrete	Average	1	No	No	No	No	Yes
Map 28 Bawley Point								
Bawley Point	Concrete	Average	1	No	No	No	No	Yes

TACKLE SHOPS ULLADULLA—MOLLYMOOK TO BAWLEY POINT

ULLADULLA SHIP SHAPE
150 Princes Highway Ulladulla
PHONE: (02) 4455 7200

ULLADULLA FISHING CENTRE
12 Wason St Ulladulla
PHONE: (02) 4455 4344

EARLY BAIT AND TACKLE
22 Watson Street Ulladulla
PHONE: (02) 4455 1938

PLAYWORLD INTERNATIONAL
119 Princes Highway Milton
PHONE: (02 4454 1555

ROBS BAIT AND TACKLE
Shop1, 105 Prince Highway Burrill Lake
PHONE: (02) 4454 3350

MACCA'S FISHING CAMPING HARDWARE
Voyager Crescent Bawley Point
PHONE: (02) 4457 1384

CHAPTER 6
BATEMANS BAY
Durras Lake to Broulee

The author with a couple of Clyde River yellowfin bream that were caught on soft plastics that were worked along the shoreline of Chinaman's Point.

Pebbly Beach is already known widely as the home of the "surfing kangaroos" (a myth arising from a photograph of a kangaroo in the low surf — probably chased there by a dog). Although they will not necessarily be surfing when you visit, you will find a large resident kangaroo population at Pebbly Beach that are quite happy to be patted or to pose for a photograph. The Pebbly Beach turnoff is located about 10 km south of Termeil and it is about 8 km in over a good gravel road to Pebbly itself.

Behind Pebbly Beach is Mount Durras, from which magnificent views over the coast and west across the hinterland to the magnificent Eastern Escarpment can be enjoyed. Mount Durras takes only about an hour to climb from Pebbly and, although quite steep in parts, is well within the capabilities of most folks.

You should also try to visit the unusual and secluded little beaches in the southern part of Murramarang National Park, reached by way of the South Durras turnoff from the highway about 20 km south of Termeil (12 km north of Batemans Bay). These beaches, with quaint names such as Emily Miller Beach, Dark Beach and others, are sandy spots in a scalloped coastline eaten out over time from these rocky shores.

Depot Beach and North Durras are small villages, mostly of holiday homes, located south of Pebbly Beach. They both offer attractive surf beaches and access to Lake Durras itself can be made from North Durras. Accommodation is available in cottages, camping and caravan parks, or you can rent one of several holiday houses. Apart from a small general store at North Durras, there are no significant services in these small villages.

South of Lake Durras, access to the village and the lake is made along the South Durras Road, which meets the Princes Highway at Benandarah, about 12 km north of Batemans Bay.

South Durras boasts several magnificent ocean beaches, access to Lake Durras and a number of accommodation options at a resort or in the local caravan and camping grounds. The access road from the highway is sealed and passes the Forest Gallery; one of the artistic highlights of the South Coast.

MAP 30 DURRAS LAKE

Durras Lake is a shallow and branching lake. The townships of Durras North and Durras Lake are located north and south of the entrance, respectively. The ocean entrance is located behind a small near shore reef which provides it with some protection from ocean waves and beach building processes.

Fishing is perhaps the most popular pastime for most visitors. Try for flathead and bream in Durras Lake, whiting, tailor and salmon off the beach, or for the more experienced, there are many rock-hopping opportunities close by.

A basic boat ramp allows for small boats to Durras Lake, but no access to the ocean. Prawning at night is also very popular during summer—a few days before and after the new moon. Durras Lake is perfect for canoeing.

If you think the environment of the Durras North area is beautiful, that's only half the story. The marine environment here is just as spectacular! Grab a mask and snorkel to experience some of the best snorkelling areas on the South Coast. There are many sheltered rock platforms nearby and at Depot and Pebbly beaches. For scuba divers, it is possible to park your car and "rock hop" many spots as well. Of course, weather and ocean conditions must always be considered before undertaking this activity.

30.1   THE ENTRANCE

When the lake is open this stretch of sand at the entrance is a great spot to fish the run-in tide for sand whiting, dusky flathead and the odd yellowfin bream. Due to the fact that the water can be so clear here I would suggest that you have a small, but steady stream of berley going as this will help keep the fish in the area you are fishing. The beach side of this sand spit is always worth a throw for bream, whiting, tailor and Australian salmon.

30.2   SCOTTY'S RUN

Anchor here close to the edge of the drop off on all tides for bream, whiting, flathead, garfish and mullet. Once again the use of berley is essential. Try having a leader that is about one to two metres in length from the swivel. This will allow the bait to move around a bit more. If you prefer to use lures and soft plastics you could try drifting your boat parallel to the shoreline and work the edge of the drop-off.

30.3   THE BOAT RAMP

Try fishing here either early in the morning or an hour or so before the sun sets for bream, whiting and flathead. I prefer to fish here with two rods when the tide is coming in. One will have a long leader from the sinker and swivel and the other rod will be rigged with a small ball sinker that will be directly down onto the top of the bait. I hold this outfit in my hand and allow the incoming tide to take the bait out to the deeper water. Very effective technique for bream.

30.4   FLATHEAD DRIFT

The name says it all. A great place to drift for dusky flathead when using bait, lures and soft plastics. Try strips of mullet, garfish, squid, tuna and half and whole pilchards when using bait. If you have never used those blade vibe lures before, you should give them a

go for flathead. Not only do they catch fish, you can get much more distance with them. This allows you to have the lure on the bottom longer.

30.5   EASTERN ARM

The eastern arm has mangroves, sand banks, weed beds and drop offs that will hold tailor, garfish, mullet, bream, dusky flathead, whiting, flounder, the odd snapper and luderick. Try drifting the area and working your baits, lures and soft plastics along the edges of this bay. If you have never experienced the thrill and excitement of catching a bream, whiting or dusky flathead on a surface lure, the edges of this bay are a great place to start trying.

30.6   THE FLATS 1

The depth of the water up in this end of the arm is very shallow, but this shouldn't deter you from fishing the area with lures and soft plastics. When the mouth is open this area can produce some very exciting fishing sessions on the surface.

30.7   WESTERN ARM

The western arm is very much like the eastern arm. It also has mangroves, sand banks, weed beds and drop offs that will hold

Durras Lake will produce tailor of this calibre during the autumn to winter months on soft plastics, hard bodied lures and small metals.

ABOVE: A great feed from Durras Lake.

Marine Sanctuary Zone

Durrass Lake

Marine Sanctuary Zone

Fish here on the run out tide for bream and flathead.

10.

Work the shallows for bream, whiting and flathead with soft plastics and lures.

9. Durras Lake

7.

5.

8. 6.

Tailor can be trolled up in these bays.

If you are going to target whiting in Durras Lakes try using either pink nippers, beach, blood, tube and squirt worms for bait. Soft plastics and poppers will also catch whiting.

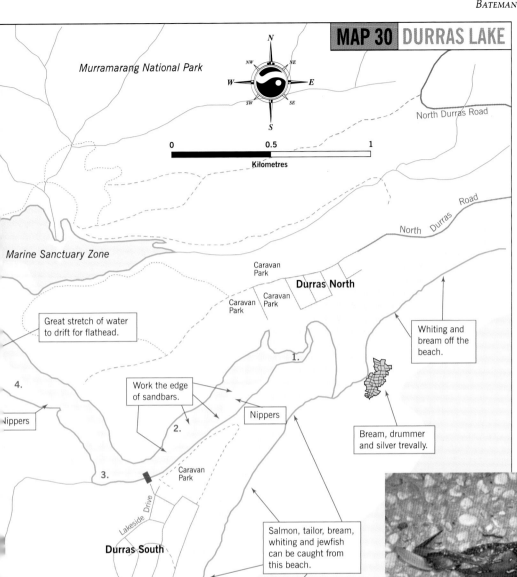

MAP 30 DURRAS LAKE

Murramarang National Park

N
NW NE
W   E
SW SE
S

0   0.5   1
Kilometres

North Durras Road

North Durras Road

Marine Sanctuary Zone

Caravan Park

Durras North

Caravan Park

Caravan Park

Great stretch of water to drift for flathead.

Whiting and bream off the beach.

4.

Work the edge of sandbars.

Nippers

1.

Nippers

2.

Bream, drummer and silver trevally.

3.

Caravan Park

Lakeside Drive

Durras South

Salmon, tailor, bream, whiting and jewfish can be caught from this beach.

---

soft plastics worked over the shallow area will also attract the bream, whiting and dusky flathead that lay in wait here.

30.9 LUDERICK CORNER

This stretch of shoreline is not a bad place to start and chase luderick during the colder months of the year. Green weed or cabbage for bait seems to get the best results, but you could also try using squirt or tube worms for bait on a long leader.

30.10 THE ISLAND

There is a combination of very shallow and deep water around this part of Durras Lake. Try working the deeper holes at low tide and then work the shallower areas as the tide is rising. It doesn't seem to matter whether you anchor or drift this part of the lake. They will both produce a few fish.

BELOW: I can't resist a feed of blue swimmer crabs.

---

tailor, garfish, mullet, bream, dusky flathead, whiting, flounder, the odd snapper and luderick. Try drifting the area and working your baits, lures and soft plastics along the edges of this bay. If you have never experienced the thrill and excitement of catching a bream, whiting or dusky flathead on a surface lure, the edges of this bay are a great place to start trying.

30.8 THE FLATS 2

The depth of the water up in this end of the arm is also very shallow and it shouldn't deter you from fishing the area with lures and soft plastics. When the mouth is open this area can produce some very exciting fishing sessions on the surface or you could try using hard bodied lures that will only swim very shallow. Lightly weighted

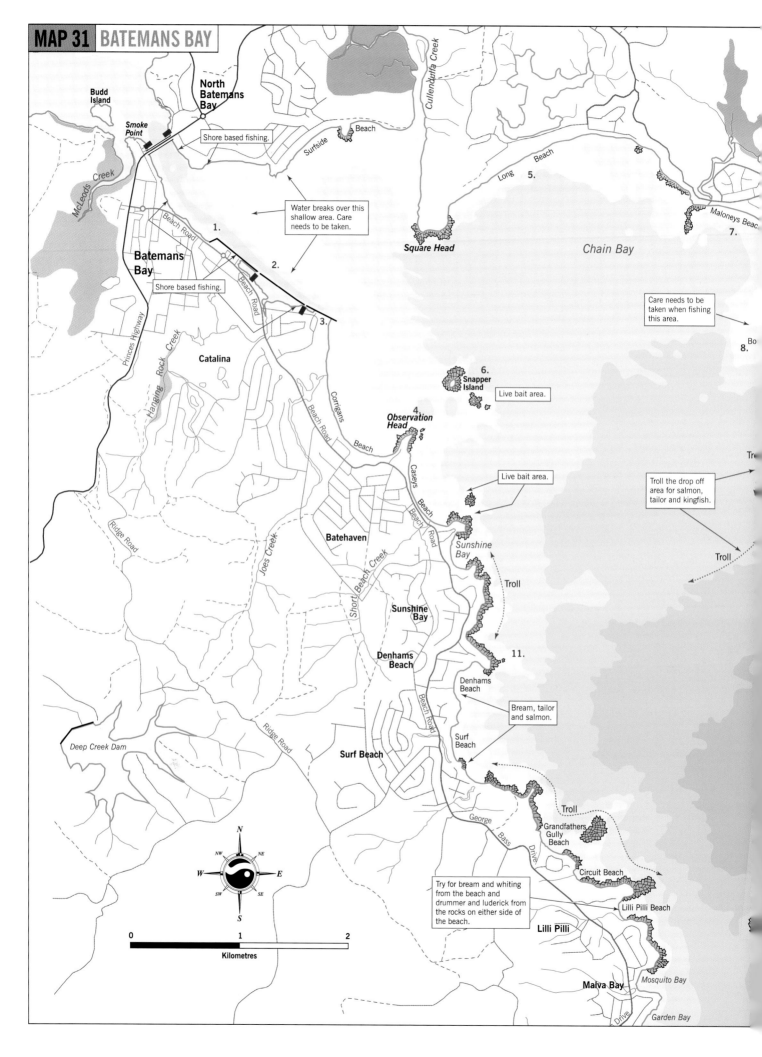

MAP 31 BATEMANS BAY

Budd
Island

North
Batemans
Bay

Smoke
Point

Shore based fishing.

Surfside Beach

Cullendulla Creek

McLeods Creek

Water breaks over this
shallow area. Care
needs to be taken.

Square Head

Chain Bay

Long Beach 5.

Maloneys Beach

7.

1.

Beach Road

Batemans
Bay

2.

Shore based fishing.

3.

Princes Highway

Hanging Rock Creek

Catalina

Corrigans Beach

Care needs to be
taken when fishing
this area.

8. Bo

4 Observation
Head

6. Snapper
Island

Live bait area.

Caseys Beach

Live bait area.

Troll the drop off
area for salmon,
tailor and kingfish.

Tr

Beach Road

Batehaven

Ridge Road

Joes Creek

Short Beach Creek

Sunshine
Bay

Sunshine
Bay

Troll

Beach Road

Troll

11.

Denhams
Beach

Denhams
Beach

Deep Creek Dam

Ridge Road

Surf Beach

Surf
Beach

Bream, tailor
and salmon.

George Bass Drive

Troll

Grandfathers
Gully Beach

Try for bream and whiting
from the beach and
drummer and luderick from
the rocks on either side of
the beach.

Circuit Beach

Lilli Pilli Beach

Lilli Pilli

Malva Bay

Mosquito Bay

Garden Bay

N
NW NE
W E
SW SE
S

0   1   2
Kilometres

MAP 31 BATEMANS BAY

Cougar
Beach

Honeysuckle
Beach

oint

North
Head
Beach

**Three Islet
Point**

North Head

Sanctuary Zone

Three Islet Reef

9.

Tollgate
Islands

Sanctuary Zone

Very shallow

0–10 m

Sand or
beach

Rocks or
boulders

Parks/National
Parks/Reserves

Swamp

BOTTOM: Skirted lures
work well for Australian
salmon when trolled in
close to the washes.

BELOW: Australian salmon
can be trolled up with
lures on the northern side
of Batemans Bay.

Fishing is fairly easy in Batemans Bay if you know a bit more about the geography of the area. First, the channel of the Clyde River passes the outside of Snapper Island and then moves south to the west of the Tollgate Islands and then midway between them and the shore. This is all a mud and sand bottom.

Secondly there are two main reefs in the area. The first one goes from the southern tip of the Tollgates and almost due east for several kilometres. The second reef begins slightly north of Black Rock and runs for several kilometres also, but in line with a few points south of east.

There is also a small reef that runs between Square Head and Chain Bay, and there is also some broken reef out from Malua Bay.

Much of these reefs are now in the sanctuary zones. Refer to the accompanying map to fully acquaint yourself with all the restrictions and areas.

31.1 STARBOARD MARKER

Work the area around the starboard marker for dusky flathead, snapper, flathead, bream and jewfish. An hour either side of the top or bottom of the tide seems to produce the better fish.

31.2 SAND SPIT

This is the sand bank that is opposite spot 31.3 and is a favourite fishing spot for bream, flathead and whiting when in season. You can either anchor here or drift along the edge of the sand bank. Tailor, snapper, mullet and garfish can also be caught here during the year. Care needs to be taken when fishing here as the bar can get very dangerous.

31.3 THE ROCK RETAINING WALL

The rock wall that runs from the mill, past the marina and out to the point has a number of prime fishing spots for both the boat and land-based angler. You can target, bream, flathead, snapper, whiting, leatherjackets and luderick on both the run-out and run-in tides. Tailor and jewfish can be targeted here after a flood or at night.

31.4 OBSERVATION HEAD

Observation Head occasionally produces good snapper, drummer, bream, tailor and kingfish. You will need to have that berley trail working to get the best results.

31.5 LONG BEACH

The fishing along this beach can be excellent at times. Target tailor, bream, whiting and flathead on a rising tide. I find that if I restrict myself to carrying one rod and a hungry bag I can become very mobile. If I am fishing a gutter and there is not much happening on this beach I can quickly move to the next gutter and not have too much to take with me. Just a small tackle box with the essentials, some bait, a knife and a bag to put the fish in.

31.6 SNAPPER ISLAND

Snapper Island is named after a ship that sheltered here. It is not a snapper spot, but you can fish here for bream and silver trevally. Care needs to be taken when fishing here as the tide does race a bit. Good place to get some of your live bait for those jewfish and kingfish.

31.7 MALONEY'S BEACH

This beach is worth a shot for bream, whiting, silver trevally, flathead and tailor on a rising tide. Good place to come when the swell is from the south and the wind is coming from the north. Some very good gutters can be found at either end of the beach. Try using a paternoster rig with beach and blood worms, pipis, pink nipper and strips of tuna or mullet for bait.

31.8 ACHERON LEDGE

Acheron Ledge is a bombora and should always be fished with caution. Big snapper, morwong, bream, tarwhine, jewfish and kingfish can be caught here on a rising tide. Try trolling for tuna, bonito, kingfish and tailor with skirted and deep diving lures.

31.9 FLATHEAD DRIFT

Drift for sand and tiger flathead at the 20 fathom mark.

31.10 MUD, REEF AND SAND LINE

This is a grey mud and sandy bottom in about 6 fathoms. Drift here for a variety of flathead. You may also come across schooling fish feeding on the surface, so it is worth putting those lures out the back for tailor, tuna and the odd kingfish.

31.11 THE LADDERS

Try trolling deep diving, surface and skirted lures for kingfish, tuna, tailor and bonito along the high rocky promontory, locally know as the Ladders. Nice drummer, bream and silver trevally can be caught in the washes around this point.

MAP 32 CLYDE RIVER

Rising in the rugged coastal mountain ranges, the river system flows south through these spectacular mountain regions, through three National Parks and no less than ten State Forests in the Clyde Valley, widening into a broad, navigable estuary and finally reaching the Pacific Ocean at Batemans Bay after a journey of around 125 km.

The Clyde opens to its estuarine state more than 30 km from its mouth at Batemans Bay and from here it is navigable for larger craft. And indeed the history of the region and its development after British settlement was based on water transport on the Clyde estuary between the towns of Batemans Bay and Nelligen.

Today it is a focus for recreational use in these towns. Sailing, river and ocean fishing, pleasure cruises, sailboards and the outboard motor boat all find their place in the extensive waterways of the estuary.

Oyster farming in the estuary is also an important industry to the local community. This is the home of the "best oysters in the world" — a claim based on the quality of the waters in which they grow, as well as the breed of oysters grown here, namely Sydney rock oysters, widely considered by the connoisseur as the best of the best.

The estuary also provides the main focus for the town of Batemans Bay. The river reaching the sea by way of the Tollgate Islands provides a backdrop to the most attractive town on the NSW south coast.

32.1 BATEMANS BAY BRIDGE

On either side of the bridge there is a concrete boat ramp. On the north-eastern side of the bridge there is a small sandy beach that is good for fishing from the shore for bream, whiting, flounder and flathead. Try using a sinker above the swivel and a one to two metre leader. The south-eastern side has a small beach that drops off into deep water. Fish here on a run-out tide for bream and flathead. You could also try anchoring in line with the bridge pylons at night for jewfish, bream and flathead. Berley will make a difference.

32.2 OYSTER RACKS

These oyster racks will at times hold good concentrations of bream, mullet, flounder, whiting, luderick and dusky flathead. Try anchoring parallel to the face of the racks, berley and use a small ball sinker down onto the hook or a swivel, sinker and a long leader.

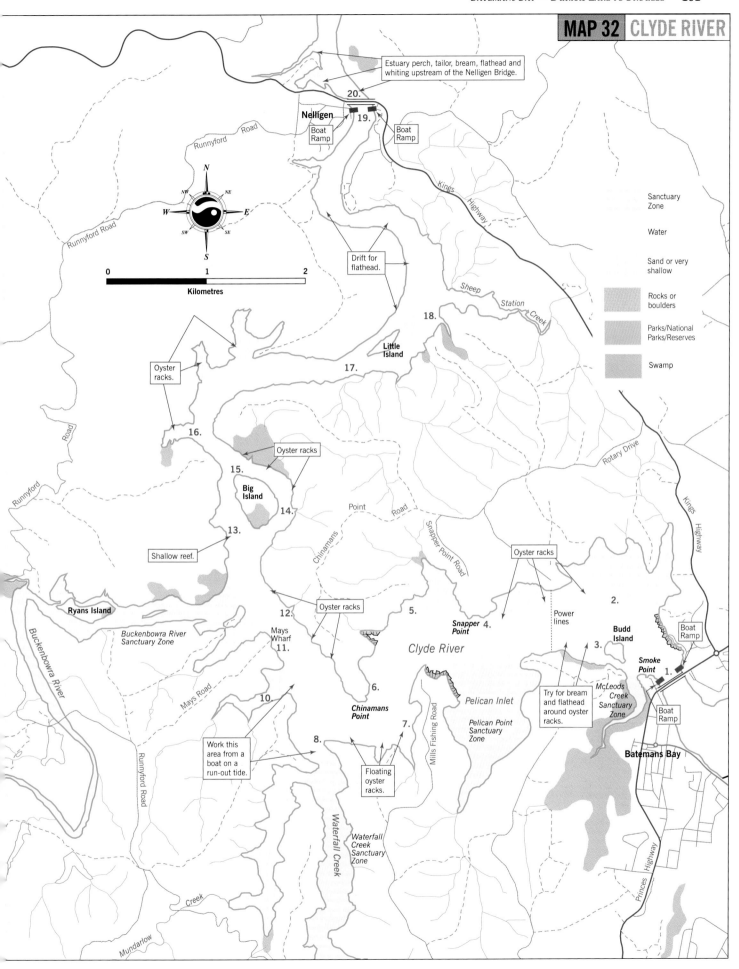

MAP 32 CLYDE RIVER

Estuary perch, tailor, bream, flathead and whiting upstream of the Nelligen Bridge.

20.

Nelligen

19.

Boat Ramp

Boat Ramp

Runnyford Road

Runnyford Road

Kings Highway

Sanctuary Zone

Water

Sand or very shallow

Rocks or boulders

Parks/National Parks/Reserves

Swamp

Drift for flathead.

Sheep Station Creek

18.

Little Island

17.

Oyster racks.

16.

Oyster racks

Rotary Drive

15.

Big Island

14.

Point Road

Chinamans Road

Snapper Point Road

Oyster racks

13.

Shallow reef.

Kings Highway

2.

Boat Ramp

Ryans Island

Buckenbowra River Sanctuary Zone

12.

Oyster racks

5.

Snapper Point 4.

Power lines

Budd Island

Smoke Point

1.

Mays Wharf

11.

Clyde River

3.

McLeods Creek Sanctuary Zone

Boat Ramp

Batemans Bay

Buckenbowra River

Mays Road

6.

Chinamans Point

7.

Pelican Inlet

Pelican Point Sanctuary Zone

Try for bream and flathead around oyster racks.

Mills Fishing Road

10.

Work this area from a boat on a run-out tide.

8.

Floating oyster racks.

Runnyford Road

Waterfall Creek

Waterfall Creek Sanctuary Zone

Princes Highway

Creek

Mundarlow

This set of racks is also worth a shot with soft plastics and hard bodied lures about an hour either side of the top of the tide. Once the tide is nearing the bottom try working the outside of the racks for dusky flathead.

32.3   BUDD ISLAND

There are fixed and floating oyster racks at the western end of the island that are in depths of water that vary from half to two metres. Try anchoring upstream of the racks at the top of the tide and fish back to the racks on the run-out tide for bream, whiting and flathead. When the tide is high you can worth those soft plastics, surface poppers and shallow diving hard bodied lures over the top of the racks. For this type of fishing you will need to upgrade your leader strength.

From the power lines to Budd Island and around the island itself are great bream and flathead spots. Jewfish, tailor and whiting can be caught here during summer.

32.4   SNAPPER POINT

The water here is fairly shallow, but the oyster racks that are found here are worth a shot for whiting, bream and flathead. Try for pan sized snapper and flounder on the drift. Directly south of Snapper Point is a mud area with numerous oyster leases. This is a prime place for bream at night. Garfish, flounder, flathead and jewfish are often taken here too. As with most spots in the river, berleying will pay dividends.

32.5   THE WASH BOARDS

The oyster racks that are in this area have wash boards to protect them. If you are bait fishing you could anchor parallel to these wash boards at high tide and fish for bream, flathead, flounder and whiting for the whole of the run-out tide. When the tide is high you can work soft plastics, surface poppers and shallow diving hard bodied lures over the top of the racks. For this type of fishing you will need to upgrade your leader strength.

32.6   CHINAMANS POINT

The point here has a combination of a rocky and sandy bottom. Fish here for silver trevally, bream, dusky flathead and the odd jewfish and snapper, on a falling tide. At high tide you can work the shallow edges with either hard bodied lures, surface poppers and lightly weighted soft plastics for bream and flathead. Between the deep hole and Snapper Point there are two reefs that project above the mud bottom at most times of the year. Good place to target jewfish, tailor and flathead with live poddy mullet.

32.7   ROCK BAR

There is a shallow rock bar that holds good fish at times. In some of the bream competitions there have been a few kilo bream taken from here. You can also fish the deeper drop-offs for flathead and legal snapper.

32.8   EDGEWOOD

Waterfall Creek entrance is home to a number of oyster racks that will hold bream, luderick, dusky flathead, leatherjackets, whiting and mullet. Don't forget that the main part of the creek is the Waterfall Creek sanctuary zone. Anchor at the edge of the zone on a run-out tide and berley the fish back up to you. You could do the same on the run-up tide.

When the tide is high you can work soft plastics, surface poppers and shallow diving hard bodied lures over the top of the racks. For this type of fishing you will need to upgrade your leader strength.

32.9   ANDREWS RACKS

Many years ago I fished this stretch of rack with a fellow by the name of Andrew. He caught more fish than me on the day that we fished it together. If I remember it was three to one. When the tide is high you can worth soft plastics, surface poppers and shallow diving hard bodied lures over the top of the racks. For this type of fishing you will need to upgrade your leader strength. When the tide is nearing the bottom, try working those lures in between the racks.

32.10   SHALLOW CREEK

There is a shallow creek here that empties into the main Clyde River that is worth fishing the whole of the falling tide for bream, flathead, whiting, flounder and snapper. At high tide you could try casting lures to the base of the mangroves that are located here.

32.11   BROKEN REEF

Shallow weedy area with a combination of racks, rock bars, sandy patches and a drop-off. Fish here for bream, flathead, leatherjackets, whiting and jewfish on the run-out tide. Work the shoreline with soft plastics and blades and allow them to get down to the bottom. Fish either early in the day or late in the afternoon.

32.12   SHALLOW REEF/ OYSTER RACKS

Shallow broken reef and oyster racks that you can drift parallel to while casting lures and soft plastics over the racks. Fish at high tide with lightly weighted soft plastics and surface poppers for bream, whiting and

There is a good population of black bream in the upper reaches of the Clyde River.

Don't those black bream look great?

flathead. You can also anchor on the outside of the racks and fish the rising tide. Don't forget to berley.

32.13   DEEP WATER POINT

Shallow broken reef and oyster racks that drop off into deep water. Fish here on the run-out tide for flathead, bream, whiting and jewfish. Make sure that you have a berley trail going.

32.14   BIG ISLAND

A good place to drift for flathead and jewfish. Try anchoring close to the shore for bream, luderick, tailor and whiting. I have found the best baits to be mullet and chicken gut, strips of mullet and tuna and live poddy mullet and pink nippers.

32.15   THE BACK CHANNEL

There is a weed bed and reef drop off into deep water at the western end of Big Island. Either anchor here and berley or deep water jig plastics and blades for bream, leatherjackets and flathead. This same area is also a good place to berley up some live bait. There are some oyster racks on the opposite side of the river that are worth a shot at the top of the tide. Drift along the edge of these oyster leases for bream, whiting and flathead. The odd jewfish has been caught here as well.

32.16   CHARLIES REACH

Good deep water rock bar that you can deep water jig soft plastics and blades for bream, flounder, snapper, flathead and jewfish. You can also try casting hard bodied lures, soft plastics and live bait in up against the mangroves that are near here.

32.17   THE HOLE

A deep hole that is approximately 100 metres downstream from Little Island that will usually hold good jewfish at times. Shallow reef and sand banks are lined with oyster racks where the channel drops off. Drift or anchor here for bream, jewfish, flathead, whiting, estuary perch, snapper and leatherjackets.

32.18   LITTLE ISLAND

There is an extensive weed bed and sand flats in this area that drop off into the channel. It is worth targeting bream, flathead, whiting and jewfish here. You could also try trolling for tailor along this stretch of water. You will come across a shallow reef and a sand bank, both lined with oyster racks. They also drop off into deep water.

32.19   NELLIGEN BRIDGE

Right at the down stream side of the bridge there is an area that is worth drifting for bream, whiting, flathead and jewfish on the run-out tide. There are two boat ramps that are located on either side of the bridge, plus a couple of wharfs.

32.20   NELLIGEN BRIDGE—UP STREAM

There is a rather large hole on the north-western side of the bridge that can hold flathead, Australian bass, estuary perch and bream. The river runs for approximately 21 km upstream to Shallow Crossing and there are plenty of places along the way where you are able to target bream, Australian bass, estuary perch and dusky flathead.

There is a seasonal closure downstream of Shallow Crossing for bass and estuary perch spawning.

BOAT RAMPS BATEMANS BAY — DURRAS LAKE TO BROULEE

Name	Make	Condition	No of Lanes	Wash Down	Lights	Fish Clean	BBQ	Toilets
Map 30 **Durras Lake**								
Ocean Parade Dalmeny	Concrete	Average	1	No	No	Yes	No	No
Durras Ocean Murramerang	Concrete	Average	1	No	No	Yes	No	Yes
Pebbly Beach North Durras	Beach sand	Poor	Nil	No	No	No	No	No
Map 31 **Bateman's Bay**								
Breakwall Caravan Park	Concrete	Excellent	4	Yes	Yes	Yes	No	No
Map 32 **Clyde River**								
North Bridge	Concrete	Poor	2	No	Yes	Yes	No	No
South Bridge	Concrete	Good	2	No	Yes	Yes	No	Yes

TACKLE SHOPS BATEMANS BAY—DURRAS LAKE TO BROULEE

HARBOUR MARINE BATEMAN'S BAY
29 Beach Rd Bateman's Bay
PHONE: (02) 4472 6869

HARRY'S BAIT & TACKLE
17 Clyde St Bateman's Bay
PHONE: (02) 4472 4393

CHARLIES TACKLEWORLD
34E Orient Street Bateman's Bay
PHONE: (02)4472 7900

COMPLEAT ANGLER
65A Orient Street Bateman's Bay
PHONE: (02) 4472 2559

TOMAKIN AUTO CENTRE
George Bass Drive Tomakin
PHONE: (02) 4471 7698

BROULEE SUPERMARKET
23-25 Grant Street Broulee
PHONE: (02) 4471 6100

AFN AUSTRALIA

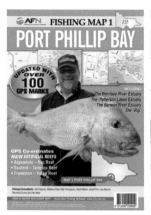

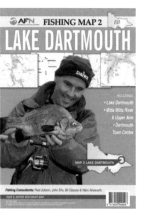

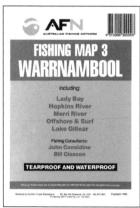

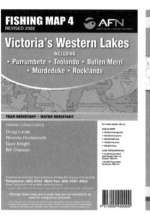

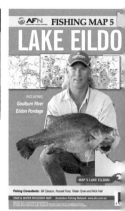

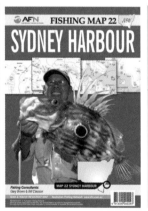

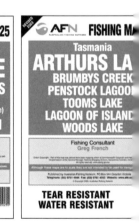

COMING SOON: MA
NORTHERN TERRIT